Pay and Pensions
for Federal Workers

Robert W. Hartman

Pay and Pensions
for Federal Workers

THE BROOKINGS INSTITUTION
Washington, D.C.

Copyright © 1983 by the Brookings Institution
1775 Massachusetts Avenue, N.W., Washington, D.C. 20036
Library of Congress Cataloging in Publication data appear on page 118.
9 8 7 6 5 4 3 2 1

Foreword

THE federal government is the nation's largest employer, but the taxpayers who foot the bill for salaries and benefits for government employees know little about the policies that guide the public payroll. Despite the general lack of information, most taxpayers have strong views about government employees and their pay. That many people think there are too many federal workers and that they are overpaid is perhaps not surprising from an electorate that often tends to hold government in low esteem. Yet uninformed prejudice is not a firm foundation on which to build a policy for federal employee compensation that is both fair and efficient.

In this study, Robert W. Hartman describes the main components of the pay and pension system for the white-collar work force of the federal government. He reviews the fundamental laws and rules that have guided pay and pensions in recent years and analyzes studies and proposals for reform of the system. The last sections of the book are devoted to detailing a plan to realign both salary and retirement benefit systems so that they will be less costly in the long run and more likely to attract and retain a qualified work force in the short run.

The study was financed in part by a grant from the Sloan Foundation. The author is grateful to Alan K. Campbell, Lily Mary David, David Delquadro, Robert J. Flanagan, and Sylvester Schieber for helpful comments. Allan Rivlin, Michael Kuehlwein, and Linda Kole provided research assistance. Vickie L. Corey, Anita G. Whitlock, and Jane R. Taylor processed the manuscript, Caroline Lalire edited it, and Judith Cameron verified its factual content. Nancy Snyder proofread the galleys and pages. Diana Regenthal prepared the index.

The views expressed are the author's alone and should not be ascribed to the Sloan Foundation, to any of those who commented on the manuscript, or to the officers, trustees, or other staff members of the Brookings Institution.

BRUCE K. MACLAURY
President

March 1983; Washington, D.C.

v

Contents

Tables

Figures

Chapter One

Introduction

THE SINGLE largest budget reduction proposed by President Ronald Reagan in his famous hit list for fiscal 1982 was the curb on federal civilian employees' pay and benefits. Outside Washington this proposal received little press or public attention, and the restraints on compensation easily passed in Congress. As budgetary pressures mount, additional proposals to restrain federal employees' compensation have come forth. Such reductions receive overwhelming public approval; yet there is probably less public knowledge about civil service pay and benefits than about any other important aspect of federal spending.

This book tries to remedy the lack of information so that public debate over federal compensation can be grounded on facts. Since one reason for the poor level of public understanding is that federal pay and benefit rules are incredibly complex and deadly boring to boot, every effort is made here to highlight only the essential facts and issues. Details are left to footnotes and appendixes.

This chapter sets out the basic facts about the civil service salary and retirement systems. It is followed by a chapter discussing problems with the salary and employment procedures. Chapter 3 raises the main issues involving the civil service retirement system. The final chapter summarizes recent reports and legislative proposals regarding compensation and presents a comprehensive reform proposal that I hope can be a starting point for serious discussion.

Trends in Employment

In fiscal 1980 federal executive branch civilian employees' pay and benefits for retired employees constituted about $73.5 billion, or 11 percent of federal obligations. Although this is a much smaller share of total spending than would be found at the state or local government

1

TABLE 1-1. *Federal Civilian Employment, Retirement, and Compensation, Selected Fiscal Years, 1960–80*

Numbers in thousands; payments in millions of dollars

Year	Executive branch civilian employment[a]		Federal retirees[b]	
	Number	Direct compensation	Number	Benefits
1960	1,818	9,812	515	767
1965	1,874	13,320	729	1,145
1970	2,205	20,913	959	2,518
1975	2,126	29,136	1,372	6,960
1980	2,270	43,254	1,675	14,551
	Annual rate of growth (percent)			
1960–65	0.6	6.3	7.2	8.3
1965–70	3.3	9.4	5.6	17.1
1970–75	−0.7	6.9	7.4	22.5
1975–80[c]	1.3	7.8	3.9	15.1

Sources: Office of Personnel Management Compensation Group, "Federal Fringe Benefit Facts, 1980" (OPM, 1981); and data provided by the Office of Personnel Management.

a. Includes both permanent and temporary full-time and part-time employees, excluding the Postal Service.

b. Civilian retired employees and survivor annuitants.

c. Covers 5.25 years, because of the change in the fiscal year in 1976.

level,[1] a change of 2 percent in an annual salary increase (or a 2 percent change in the employment level) is a $1 billion decision.

About 2.3 million employees received $43.3 billion in salaries, overtime, and other forms of direct compensation (thus averaging about $19,000 per worker), and 1.7 million retirees received $15 billion in retirement benefits (about $9,000 per retiree). The rest of the expenditures went for health and life insurance benefits.

Trends in these costs are shown in table 1-1. The level of employment remained remarkably stable from 1960 through 1980, while the total federal budget almost doubled in real terms over the period. Payroll costs, nonetheless, rose sharply, with payroll per worker going up 76 percent in the 1960s and 101 percent in the 1970s. By contrast, the growth in outlays for employees' retirement was due much more to the growth in numbers of recipients, which rose 86 percent in the sixties and 75 percent in the seventies. (This rapid growth reflected the vast increase in federal civilian employment during the depression and World War II:

1. For example, in 1980, 53 percent of state and local government expenditures went to employee compensation.

in 1929 federal employment stood at 560,000 people; in 1945 at 3,800,000.)[2]
Retirement benefits per recipient grew even faster than payroll per
worker, increasing 76 percent in the 1960s and 231 percent in the 1970s.

The relatively slow growth in federal employment in the 1960s and
1970s was the result of various changes in the government's activities.
The most important thing to remember is that the direct provision of
services (for example, medical care in a Veterans Administration hos-
pital) by the federal government is a labor-intensive activity, while
indirect provision of services (say, through grants-in-aid for medicaid)
or income support (social security) uses fewer employees per dollar of
expenditure. Of all the federal government's major functions, the provision of national defense is the heaviest user of civilian (and, obviously,
military) manpower. For instance, in fiscal 1980 the national defense
budget constituted about 23 percent of all federal spending, yet the
Department of Defense employed 41 percent of all full-time and part-
time civilian employees.[3] As the data in table 1-2 show, there was a
massive shift in the federal budget between 1960 and 1980, in which
national defense declined from 49 percent to 23 percent of spending.
This reduction allowed the "release" of 86,000 civilian employees of the
Department of Defense. The 535,000 additional employees needed to
accommodate the spectacularly growing nondefense sector, therefore,
was partly offset by the reduced national defense work force.

Within the nondefense sector, the most rapid growth was in grants-
in-aid to state and local governments, the more categorical of which
(that is, those in which the grant is based on an evaluation of project
proposals) are fairly labor intensive at the federal level, and direct
transfers, such as social security, which are not labor intensive. Relative
declines occurred in net interest, a very low labor-using activity, and in
"other," the category that includes many direct services of federal
agencies (national park operators, air traffic control, veterans' medical
service, and so on) that are quite labor intensive. In all, the shifts within
the nondefense sector had probably less effect on employment than the
defense-to-nondefense shift.

The Reagan administration has begun a dramatic reordering of budget
priorities, with the national defense share of the budget programmed to
rise to 38 percent of total federal spending by 1986 (table 1-2). Should

2. These data include Postal Service employees.
3. Spending and employment data exclude the civil functions (primarily Corps of
Engineers) in the Department of Defense.

TABLE 1-2. *Defense and Nondefense Shares of the Federal Budget, Selected Fiscal Years, 1960–86*

Item	1960	1970	1980	1986[a]
Defense				
Expenditures (billions of dollars)	45.2	78.6	135.9	343.0
Percent of total budget	49.0	40.0	23.0	38.0
Civilian employment (millions)[b]	1.0	1.2	0.9	c
Percent of total civilian				
employment	56.0	56.0	41.0	c
Nondefense				
Expenditures (billions of dollars)	47.1	118.0	443.8	612.0
Percent of total budget	51.0	60.0	77.0	62.0
Civilian employment (millions)	0.8	1.0	1.3	c
Percent of total civilian				
employment	44.0	44.0	59.0	c
Composition of nondefense				
expenditures (percent)				
Grants-in-aid	15.0	20.0	21.0	15.0
Direct transfers	45.0	46.0	53.0	65.0
Net interest	15.0	12.0	12.0	10.0
Other	25.0	22.0	14.0	10.0
Total	100.0	100.0	100.0	100.0

Sources: Office of Management and Budget, "Federal Government Finances" (March 1981), pp. 65, 69; and data provided by the Office of Personnel Management.
a. Projections do not include unspecified future budget savings.
b. Number of full-time equivalent employees in the Department of Defense with military functions.
c. Projections not available.

past practice hold true, this shift will significantly increase the civilian work force in the Department of Defense. Whether the nondefense program cuts, also promoted by the Reagan plan, will entail enough employment reductions in nondefense agencies to offset the defense increase seems, however, problematic. The program reductions in the 1982 (first Reagan) budget were heavily concentrated on reducing the dollar volume of grant-in-aid and transfer programs, which implies hardly any change in employment.[4] President Reagan's proposals for grant consolidation, which would reduce the federal work force, were only partly accepted by Congress. Future reductions in nondefense spending are likely to involve benefit cutbacks in social insurance programs that will create little employment saving. But some employment reduction should result from deregulation efforts, since fewer, less-detailed rules

4. See Congressional Budget Office, *An Analysis of the President's Budgetary Proposals for Fiscal Year 1983* (Government Printing Office, 1982).

or reduced enforcement requires fewer workers. Unless future budgets trim back the heavy labor-using activities in the nondefense budget—the provision of services—budget reductions in primarily check-writing activities of the government will not provide enough released labor to offset the increases in national defense. It appears, then, that given the new budget priorities, it will be difficult to limit federal work-force costs by reducing employment levels. Attention must therefore be paid to salaries and to nonsalary benefits as sources of economies.[5]

Salary Structure of the White-Collar Work Force

Up to now my description of federal civilian employees has failed to distinguish between various subgroups. But to understand the salary structure of federal employees, one must distinguish at least four groups, because their pay is set differently. These groups are (1) general schedule workers, (2) senior executives, (3) executive schedule workers, and (4) blue-collar workers. The blue-collar workers are predominantly in the Defense Department, and their pay system warrants specialized treatment beyond the scope of this study.[6]

General Schedule

Most of the white-collar work force is employed under the general schedule. Moreover, many other white-collar positions have pay systems identical or closely related to the general schedule. Table 1-3 shows the relative proportions of employees under these systems.

STRUCTURE. The general schedule pay system is job-based. Every position in the federal government is assigned an occupational series code, which amounts to an occupational title. For example, chemist (code 1320: 8,083 positions in 1980), secretary (code 318: 79,470 posi-

5. I do not mean to downplay the possibility of curbing employment by fostering greater productivity in the federal work force. Such measures are obviously important. But I am skeptical of the government's ability—short of an all-out managerial revolution—to effect large savings from increased productivity.

6. In 1980 over 70 percent of blue-collar workers were in the Department of Defense. For a discussion of blue-collar pay problems, see Congressional Budget Office, *Alternative Approaches to Adjusting Compensation for Federal Blue-Collar Employees* (GPO, 1980). In addition, Postal Service workers are paid under two other pay systems, which were created by the Postal Reorganization Act of 1970 and together cover some 560,000 postal workers.

TABLE 1-3. *Federal Civilian Employment and Payroll by Pay System, Executive Branch, Fiscal Year 1980*

Pay system	Employees (thousands)[a]	Payroll (millions of dollars)
Wage system (blue collar)	456.6	8,187
White collar	1,514.9	30,717
General schedule	1,402.2	27,918
Senior Executive Service	6.8	342
Executive schedule	0.4	24
Other related pay systems[b]	105.5	2,433

Source: Office of Personnel Management, "Work Years and Personnel Costs, Executive Branch, Fiscal Year 1980" (OPM, 1981).

a. In work years—that is, time actually paid for; two half-time employees count as one, and unfilled positions are not counted.

b. Includes such systems as the foreign service, Tennessee Valley Authority, general grades, and Department of Medicine and Surgery in the Veterans Administration.

tions in 1980), and personnel manager (code 201: 10,367 positions in 1980). Altogether there are about 450 occupations. Within each occupational series different work levels are identified according to level of responsibility, complexity of tasks, number of employees supervised or (in the case of secretaries) level of responsibility of supervisor, and so on. All told, with five to six work levels for each occupation there are some 2,600 jobs to be assigned salaries.

Each work level of each occupation is then assigned to one of fifteen general schedule grades: GS-1 to GS-15; GS-1 being the lowest.[7] Thus, for example, over 90 percent of secretarial positions are in GS-4–9, chemists are found mainly in GS-7–14, and personnel directors are bunched in GS-9–15. Each general schedule grade is assigned a salary range, as shown in table 1-4 for March 1981. The lower fifth of the employees, those in grades 1–4, are largely in clerical occupations; about 75 percent are women. The middle grades, GS-5–10, comprise 45 percent of the white-collar work force, in jobs that are about half in upper-level clerical and technical work levels and half in low-to-medium professional and administrative levels; women make up about half the work force in these jobs. The upper level of the general schedule, paying an average salary of over $25,000 in grades GS-11–15, has about 35 percent of the slots, almost all of which are in professional and administrative occupations; women held about one-seventh of these jobs in 1980.[8]

7. There are actually eighteen GS grades, but almost all positions in the GS-16–18 range have been reclassified into the Senior Executive Service.

8. Data on occupation and sex from Office of Personnel Management, *Occupations of Federal White-Collar Workers, October 31, 1980* (GPO, 1980).

TABLE 1-4. *General Schedule Salaries and Employment Distribution, March 1981*

Dollars unless otherwise specified

Grade level	Salary range	Estimated average salary[a]	Percent of GS employment
1	7,960–9,954	8,074	0.2
2	8,951–11,265	9,149	1.7
3	9,766–12,700	10,434	6.4
4	10,963–14,248	12,174	12.2
5	12,266–15,947	13,912	13.6
6	13,672–17,776	15,741	6.3
7	15,193–19,747	17,172	9.4
8	16,826–21,875	19,531	2.0
9	18,585–24,165	20,862	9.9
10	20,467–26,605	23,206	2.0
11	22,486–29,236	25,464	11.0
12	26,951–32,033	30,325	11.4
13	32,048–41,660	36,665	7.9
14	37,871–49,229	43,249	4.1
15	44,547–57,912	50,113[b]	2.0

Sources: William M. Davis, "U.S. General Schedule Employees Received 9.1-Percent Salary Increase in October 1980," *Current Wage Developments*, vol. 33 (January 1981), p. 45; and data provided by the Office of Personnel Management. Figures are rounded.

a. Estimated by applying the October 1980 pay increase to the average grade salaries of March 31, 1980.

b. Actual salary paid is limited by statutory ceiling.

The range of salary in each GS grade is divided into ten equal steps. The salary at each step is increased by 3.3 percent of the step 1 level, the lowest in the grade. Ordinarily an employee starts in step 1 and advances one step every year (steps 2–4), or every two years (steps 5–7), or every three years (steps 8–10). No longevity increases are given once step 10 is reached. Although such step increases are not automatic and may be withheld for unsatisfactory performance, in over 90 percent of the cases they are granted. The significance of the longevity increases is that a given worker can expect two sources of salary increase in a federal job: a step increase of about 3 percent every other year, on average, plus any increase in the general schedule rates of pay.[9] (The latter is what the media report when they say that pay raises were *x* percent.) Step increases also imply that the pay of two federal workers in identical jobs may vary by 30 percent, depending on time-in-grade.

9. In 1980, 39 percent of employees were eligible for annual step increases, 31 percent for increases at two-year intervals, and 21 percent had a three-year wait. Eight percent were at the top step. These data include a small number of employees in grades 16–18. Data from Office of Personnel Management, *Pay Structure of the Federal Civil Service, March 31, 1980*, Federal Civilian Work Force Statistics (GPO, 1980).

The federal general schedule payroll at any time, therefore, depends on the number of employees, the pay rates for each grade, the grade structure of the work force, and the step-in-grade structure. The effect of each of these on costs is described in the next two subsections.

CHANGES IN SALARY SCHEDULES.[10] The statutory basis for establishing federal pay rates is the Federal Pay Comparability Act of 1970. That act stipulates that "pay distinctions be maintained in keeping with work . . . distinctions" (internal alignment) and that "federal pay rates be comparable with private enterprise pay rates for the same levels of work" (external alignment, or pay comparability).[11]

To implement the pay comparability standard, the Bureau of Labor Statistics (BLS) annually conducts a survey of private sector pay rates for professional, administrative, technical, and clerical jobs (the PATC survey).[12] At each federal GS level certain jobs are singled out and matched with private sector jobs that experts have judged to be comparable in duties and responsibilities. Average salaries are then computed for these private sector jobs at each federal GS level by using the survey data on the matched jobs.[13]

Table 1-5 illustrates some of the variation in salaries in the private sector for jobs that are equivalent to federal jobs in GS-5. Clerical positions, which account for about 60 percent of all PATC jobs in grade 5, are paid much lower salaries in the private sector, according to the BLS survey, than "equivalent" professional or administrative jobs. But in the federal work force, all GS-5 jobs are paid the same, with the slight variation by occupation (table 1-5) dependent only on time-in-grade.[14]

10. Some parts of this section are drawn from Robert W. Hartman, "The Effects of Top Officials' Pay on Other Federal Employees," in Robert W. Hartman and Arnold R. Weber, eds., *The Rewards of Public Service: Compensating Top Federal Officials* (Brookings Institution, 1980), p. 203.

11. 5 U.S.C. 5301.

12. The survey is described and reported annually by the U.S. Bureau of Labor Statistics as *National Survey of Professional, Administrative, Technical, and Clerical Pay*. For further details on comparability techniques, see Congressional Budget Office, *The Federal Government's Pay Systems: Adjustment Procedures and Impacts of Proposed Changes*, Background Paper 19 (GPO, 1977).

13. The weights used to determine averages are the numbers of federal employees in the occupational categories represented by matched jobs in the survey. In 1980 about 92 percent of all federal jobs up to GS-15 were so represented.

14. Clerical workers in grade 5 are usually in a middle career position (for example, secretary II is secretary to a supervisor whose unit's "organizational structure is complex and is divided into subordinate groups"), whereas professionals often enter government at this grade (for example, chemist I is "the entry level . . . requiring a bachelor's

TABLE 1-5. *Comparison between Private and Federal Salaries for Jobs Equivalent to General Schedule Grade 5, March 1980*
Dollars unless otherwise specified

Occupational category	Private sector	Federal	Percent difference
Total professional	16,557	12,254	35.1
Chemist I	16,200	11,550	40.3
Total administrative	15,020	12,307	22.0
Job analyst I	16,056	12,698	26.4
Total technical	14,900	12,626	18.0
Computer operator II	12,016	12,441	− 3.4
Total clerical	12,740	12,900	− 1.2
Secretary II	12,611	12,963	− 2.7
All categories	13,606	12,733	6.8

Sources: *Comparability of the Federal Statutory Pay Systems with Private Enterprise Pay Rates: Annual Report of the President's Pay Agent, 1980;* and data provided by the Office of Personnel Management.

The technique for determining comparability increases for the fifteen matched-job grades is as follows. A smooth curve is first fitted through the average-salary-by-grade points derived from the BLS survey. This "survey pay-line" curve is estimated by regression techniques that place the greatest weight on GS grades with the largest number of employees. Because of this weighting the curve may deviate from the actual survey averages by a considerable margin in GS categories having few represented employees.[15] The mathematical form of the curve used—out of many possible forms—is one in which intergrade percentage differences gradually diminish.[16]

A curve of identical mathematical form is then fitted through the data on actual average GS salaries in each grade. This "reference line" also is based on the principle of making the curve fit the heavily populated GS levels most closely, and it also has had the characteristic of diminishing intergrade percentage differences.

The percentage pay increase for comparability is then found by calculating the percentage difference between the survey pay line and

degree in Chemistry and no experience"). Thus clericals remain longer in this grade and reach a higher step than professionals, who would ordinarily be promoted to a higher grade. Quotations are from Bureau of Labor Statistics, *National Survey*, BLS Bulletin 2108 (GPO, 1981), pp. 52, 68.

15. In the 1980 survey about 80 percent of the employment weights were between GS-4 and GS-12.

16. The form of the equation is $W_g = ab^i c^{i^2}$, where W_g is average salary in grade g; a, b, c are constants to be estimated; and i is a grade index. (Since promotions up to

TABLE 1-6. *Computation of Recommended 1980 Pay Increases by Comparability Method, Selected General Schedule Levels*
Dollars unless otherwise specified

	General schedule		BLS survey		Percent difference	
GS level	Average salary	Reference line	Average salary	Pay line	Between averages	Between lines
1	7,122	7,644	8,110	8,668	13.9	13.4
3	9,551	9,835	11,254	11,030	17.8	12.2
5	12,733	12,485	13,606	13,912	6.9	11.4
7	15,723	15,637	18,107	17,390	15.2	11.2
9	19,105	19,322	22,183	21,543	16.1	11.5
11	23,324	23,555	26,585	26,451	14.0	12.3
13	33,583	33,620	38,278	38,821	14.0	15.5
15	47,116	45,465	53,956	54,971	14.5	20.9
Average[a]	19,577	19,583	22,211	22,201	13.5	13.4

Source: *Annual Report of the President's Pay Agent, 1980*, p. 19.
a. Average of grades 1–15 weighted by government employment.

the reference line at each GS level (table 1-6). For example, the GS-5 increase in 1980 under comparability is 11.4 percent, the difference between $13,912, the GS-5 salary computed from the pay line, and $12,485, the GS-5 salary computed from the reference line.[17] This comparability increase, it should be noted, may differ considerably from a pay adjustment based on simply observing the difference between the survey average and the actual average GS pay (6.9 percent in this example). The main effect of using the reference line and survey pay line is to smooth the pay raises across grades.

The last step in the comparability methodology is to apply the

---

GS-11 are typically "double grade"—for example, from GS-5 to GS-7—and each GS level above grade 11 represents a promotion, the grade index used in the computation is $i = g$ for $g = 1, 2, 3, \ldots 11$; $i = 13, 15, 17, 19$ for $g = 12, 13, 14, 15$.) In each of the last three years the estimate of the parameter b has been slightly above one and that of c slightly below one. Since the percentage difference between grades 1 and 2 in the equation is equal to $bc^3 - 1$ and that between grades 2 and 3 is equal to $bc^5 - 1$, and so on, the intergrade percentage difference diminishes as long as c is less than one. The regression technique used to estimate the parameters amounts to first rewriting the equation in logarithmic form and then finding (by standard regression methods) the parameters that minimize the weighted sum of the squared logarithms of the deviations of the data from the curve.

17. The parameters a, b, and c (see note 16) for 1980 were as follows: for the survey pay line, $7,658, 1.1331, and 0.9989, respectively; for the reference line, $6,705, 1.1420, and 0.9983, respectively.

percentage increases derived from the curves (last column in table 1-6) to the step 1 salary rates of the previous period in each grade. Thus in 1980 the GS pay schedule would have been shifted up by a low of about 11 percent in grade 7 to a high of 21 percent in grade 15.[18] It should be noted that the comparability increase of 11.4 percent for GS-5s would raise clerical pay to well above the private sector level of March and be inadequate for professional, administrative, and technical occupations in that grade (see table 1-5). Since comparability increases, based on March data, go into effect in October of each year, there is always a lag in federal pay.

All these comparability changes are what the federal statutes require unless the president submits, and Congress does not reject, an alternate plan. In the last six years, Congress has accepted an alternate plan. A chronology of these pay schedule changes, shown in table 1-7, indicates that only in 1976 was pay comparability enforced. In the five subsequent salary schedule adjustments an equal percent increase was applied across-the-board to all GS grades. In 1977 the across-the-board percentage was equal to the average derived from the comparability exercise. In 1978, 1979, 1980, and 1981 the pay increase was held below the average comparability change. The net result of the recent departures from comparability is that a large and growing gap between pay comparability and actual pay levels has been created, especially at the upper end of the GS grade spectrum.

One new feature of the federal pay system, which has not yet been implemented, may mitigate shortfalls at the GS-13–15 level. Under the Civil Service Reform Act of 1978, managers in grades 13–15 will automatically receive only one-half of the scheduled increase for their grade and step each October. The remaining half of the salary boost in each agency's budget will be put into a pool for the payment of "merit pay increases" to these managers. A manager may receive a bonus of up to 20 percent of basic salary in any year. There is, however, no merit pay plan for nonmanagers in grades 13–15, most of whom are scientists, engineers, and analysts.

SOURCES OF GROWTH IN SALARIES. The contribution of the various determinants of general schedule employees' salary to payroll growth from 1970 to 1980 is summarized in table 1-8. The annualized GS payroll rose about 80 percent over the decade, with a somewhat faster rate of

18. The pay increases for grades 1 and 2 were distorted by a discontinuity in pay rates for below-minimum-wage workers as a result of wage guidelines in 1979.

TABLE 1-7. *General Schedule Salary Changes under Pay Comparability and the President's Alternate Plan for Selected Grades, 1976–81*

Percent increase

Date	Pay comparability				Alternate plan			
	Average	GS-5	GS-11	GS-15	Average	GS-5	GS-11	GS-15
October 1976	5.17	4.24	4.93	7.92	5.17	4.24	4.93	7.92
October 1977[a]	7.05	6.34	6.67	9.85	7.05	7.05	7.05	7.05
October 1978	8.40	6.40	8.17	13.27	5.50	5.50	5.50	5.50
October 1979	10.41	8.86	9.70	15.43	7.00	7.00	7.00	7.00
October 1980	13.49	11.42	12.30	20.91	9.10	9.10	9.10	9.10
October 1981	15.10	12.08	4.21	23.33	4.80	4.80	4.80	4.80

Sources: *Annual Report of the President's Pay Agent*, 1977–81; and data provided by the Office of Personnel Management.
a. The actual recommendation by the President's Pay Agent was a 7.05 percent across-the-board increase.

TABLE 1-8. *Components of Change in the Annualized Federal Payroll, 1970–80*[a]

Percent increase

Source of change	1970–75[b]		1975–80[b]	
	Absolute contribu- tion	Relative contribu- tion	Absolute contribu- tion	Relative contribu- tion
Employment	4.9	13.1	3.2	7.5
Pay schedule	30.0	80.0	33.5	78.1
Grade increase	1.0	2.7	3.2	7.5
Other[c]	1.6	4.3	3.0	7.0
Total annualized salary	37.5	100.0	42.9	100.0

Sources: U.S. Civil Service Commission, *Pay Structure of the Federal Civil Service, March 31, 1970* (Government Printing Office, 1971), and ibid., *March 31, 1975* (GPO, 1976); Davis, "U.S. General Schedule Employees"; and worksheet from the Office of Personnel Management of PATCO (professional, administrative, technical, clerical, and other). Figures are rounded.

a. Full-time general schedule employees in grades 1–15 as of March 31 each year.

b. Calculated by starting with the formula

$$AGSAL = EMP(MSAL_i \cdot STEP_i \cdot GRADE_i),$$

where *AGSAL* is aggregate salary, *EMP* is the total number of GS-1–15 employees, *MSAL* is the minimum (step 1) salary in each grade, *STEP* is the ratio of the average to the minimum salary in each grade, and *GRADE* is the employment distribution by grade. The later year component is substituted for the base year component to determine the contribution of each source. The *MSAL* change in each grade represents the general salary scale's effect.

c. Includes the effects of "step creep" and compounding.

growth in 1975–80 than in 1970–75.[19] The increase in the general schedule salary scale itself contributed about 80 percent of the total payroll increase throughout the decade. Employment growth accounted for about 10 percent of payroll growth, but this source decelerated sharply in the second half of the decade. It is interesting to note that "grade creep"—the increase in the average grade of GS employment—shifted sharply upward in the second half of the decade, accounting for 7.5 percent of payroll growth. In the 1975–80 period, when the average GS grade level rose from 7.9 to 8.2, about 0.6 percent ($170 million a year at 1980 salary levels) was being added to payroll each year from this source. Other factors, including a small upward increase in the average step within most grades, accounted for the rest of the payroll increase.

Senior Executive Service and Executive Schedule

Near the top of the federal employee work force is the 6,600-person Senior Executive Service. And at the pinnacle are the roughly 350

19. The annualized salary payroll is the product of full-time employment at mid-year (March) and the full-year salary for each grade and step of the general schedule.

executive branch officials whose pay is governed by the executive schedule. This is not the place for a full discussion of the compensation system for these two groups,[20] but the linkages with the general schedule pay should be noted here.

The executive schedule covers political appointees ranging from cabinet-level secretaries of departments (executive level I) to deputy assistant secretaries and equivalent positions (executive level V). The executive schedule level V salary is, by law, the ceiling on salary rates for the general schedule. According to law, pay rates for these executive positions are to be adjusted annually by the same average percent increase as the general schedule, and every four years a presidential commission may propose major modifications in executive pay. In practice, executive pay rates are frozen for long intervals.[21] A large increase in executive pay rates was granted in March 1977. But between then and the middle of 1981, only one increase of 5.5 percent was granted, in October 1979, when the salary for executive level V went from $47,500 to $50,113. Since GS salaries rose about 32 percent between 1977 and 1980, while the ceiling rose by only 5.5 percent, more and more white-collar workers had their pay determined by the ceiling. In early 1981 all GS workers above grade 15, level 5, received the same $50,113 rate of pay. It is estimated that when all related pay systems are taken into account, as many as 33,500 federal workers (including the Senior Executive Service) were then "compressed" at the same salary.[22]

The Senior Executive Service was established in 1979, largely as a replacement for grades 16–18 (supergrades) in the general schedule. Its members are mostly (at least 85 percent) career employees.[23] The pay system for this elite corps was intended to be fundamentally different from that of the general schedule, where jobs are assigned a grade level and qualified people are then found for the job. The SES is a graded

20. See Hartman and Weber, eds., *Rewards of Public Service*, for a full discussion.
21. See *Report of the Commission on Executive, Legislative, and Judicial Salaries, December 1980* (GPO, 1980).
22. In the last congressional action of 1981 the ceiling on GS pay was raised 14 percent, to $57,500. Though this helped a little, many managers are still at the pay cap.
23. The career members of the SES are the closest analogy to the top-level civil servants who "run the government" in parliamentary democracies. The uniquely American contribution to public administration—many layers of short-term political appointees—is found in the executive schedule or among noncareer members of the SES. Hugh Heclo, *A Government of Strangers: Executive Politics in Washington* (Brookings Institution, 1977).

system (the Civil Service Reform Act specifies "5 or more levels of basic pay"; there are currently six grades) in which a member is ranked according to his experience, training, and skills. Once ranked, a member can be assigned any managerial job in his agency.[24]

Pay for the SES consists of two main elements. The first is basic pay, which is the salary assigned to the rank within the SES. The second is "performance awards," a system of bonuses to be given to no more than 50 percent of the (career) SES members in any year and to be limited to no more than 20 percent of basic pay.[25] In this pay system basic salary (and rank) are essentially backward-looking—how impressive is the member's curriculum vitae?—whereas bonuses are a reward for specific service rendered "with distinction" recently.

The links of SES pay to other pay systems have prevented it from being fully implemented. The law limits pay for the SES by setting the minimum basic pay rate at GS-16, step 1, and the maximum at executive level IV. Until 1980 the GS-16, step 1 level was derived by extrapolating the pay-line curves used to calculate comparability. Such an extrapolation in October 1980 would have yielded a pay rate of $59,653, which was in excess of the executive V ($50,113) limit on general schedule pay.

The maximum rate for the SES in 1980, limited to the frozen level for executive level IV, was set at $52,750, but certain limitations in the appropriations acts effectively limited all but a few persons to the top basic pay of $50,113. Thus, in fiscal 1981 the six ranks of SES members earned the same basic salary without any variation to cover differences in skill, training, and experience.[26]

The bonus system in the SES was also limited to less than is permissible in the enabling legislation. In 1980, when a few agencies began to announce bonuses to nearly 50 percent of their SES employees, members of the House of Representatives offered legislation that threatened to

24. This shift to "rank in person" was intended to eliminate some rigidities of the previous supergrade system, in which some employees virtually "owned" their jobs. Under the SES they own their rank but can be transferred to other jobs in the same way that a professor of English can be assigned to teach freshman writing without being demoted.

25. A third element of SES compensation is more like a prize. Up to 5 percent of the SES can be designated "meritorious executives" and another 1 percent "distinguished executives," receiving a lump-sum payment of $10,000 and $20,000, respectively.

26. Finally, in December 1981 the executive level IV ceiling was raised to $58,500, and the salary range for the SES became $54,755 to $58,500, still rather narrow for six ranks.

scrap the bonuses altogether. A compromise with the Senate restricted awards to no more than 25 percent of the eligible members. Working under that guideline, agencies paid bonuses in 1980 to 23 percent of the SES members, with an average award of about 11 percent of basic pay.[27]

Pay for the executive level and for the SES, however, is not a serious budgetary issue. Combined payroll for all these officials in fiscal 1982 was about $350 million, or 0.05 percent of federal outlays in that year.

Civil Service Retirement

White-collar workers employed under the general schedule participate in the civil service retirement (CSR) system, a program set up in 1920. As a result, when social security was established in the mid-1930s, federal civil servants were not included in that national social insurance plan. Today federal civilian employees, including members of Congress and employees of the Social Security Administration, are the largest group excluded from social security.[28] The pensions received from CSR, therefore, should not be compared with private pensions alone, which are almost always complemented by social security.

To be eligible for "voluntary" retirement with full annuity, a federal employee must have worked thirty years and attained the age of fifty-five or worked twenty years and reached age sixty.[29] If a federal employee quits anytime after having served five years, but before becoming eligible for a full annuity, he can receive a deferred annuity when he reaches sixty-two, or he may choose to receive a lump-sum refund of his contributions with no interest.

The amount of the annuity is based on the number of years of service and on salary. Since 1969 salary used in the annuity computation is the

27. In 1981 a typical SES member whose basic pay was $50,113 and who received the maximum (20 percent) bonus made $60,135. Congressmen and senators were paid $60,663. These figures are not unrelated. See Hartman, "Effects of Top Officials' Pay," pp. 203–29.

28. Federal military personnel are included in social security; about 30 percent of state and local government employees are not included. Department of Health, Education, and Welfare, Universal Social Security Coverage Study Group, "Report: The Desirability and Feasibility of Social Security Coverage for Employees of Federal, State and Local Governments and Private Non Profit Organizations" (March 1980), pp. 151, 161.

29. Various other provisions cover employees who are separated "not for cause." For example, a worker with twenty-five years of service (including military service) may receive an annuity at any age if he is fired. The annuity is reduced by 2 percent for each year below age fifty-five.

"high-3," the highest average salary during any three consecutive years of employment. For full-career workers these are ordinarily the last three years before retirement. Each of the first five years of service earns a 1.5 percent credit for the worker; each of the next five earns him or her 1.75 percent, and each year of service above ten adds another 2 percent. The annuity is computed by summing the credits for years of service and multiplying by the high-3. The maximum annuity is 80 percent of the high-3.

Thus, for example, a clerical employee retiring after thirty years' service at age fifty-five in 1980 with a high-3 average salary of $16,000 (this would be a GS-8 worker with a final year salary of about $17,360) would receive an annuity of $9,000. The thirty years of service result in credits of 56.25 percent, which is multiplied by $16,000 to determine the pension. Since the last year's salary is ordinarily higher than the high-3 because of GS schedule increases and step increases, the ratio of pension to final salary (the "replacement rate") will be less than 56.25 percent for thirty years of service. As a rough measure, a thirty-year career will bring federal employees a replacement rate a little above 50 percent. This replacement rate depends only on length of service: a thirty-year federal employee whose high-3 average is double or half that of the clerical worker will also receive a replacement rate of about half of final salary. After thirty-five years of service, replacement rates would be about 60 percent; after forty-two years of service, the maximum pension, amounting to about 75 percent of final salary, is attainable.

Once the former federal employee begins to draw a pension, it is adjusted for the cost of living every six months. Each March increase is based on the rise in the consumer price index (CPI) from the preceding June–December period, and each September adjustment is based on the preceding December–June rise. This indexing system, begun in 1977, replaced the more generous one prevailing between 1969 and 1976, which provided for cost-of-living adjustments plus 1 percent every time the CPI rose by 3 percent. In 1981 Congress voted to limit the indexation further by reducing the frequency of adjustments to once a year beginning in 1982.

Civil service retirement participants have contributed 7 percent of their entire salary to the system each year since 1970.[30] Before that the rate was 6.5 percent from 1956 through 1969 and 6 percent from 1948

---

30. Congressmen and legislative employees, who may voluntarily participate in CSR, contribute 7.5 percent, but they accumulate service credits at a faster rate.

through 1955. In general, the civil service employees' retirement contribution has always been much larger than employees' social security contributions, especially at the upper end of the income scale, where social security taxes are limited by a maximum.

CSR benefits are taxable according to the same rules as apply to private pension plans. Benefits that represent a return of the employee's contributions are not taxed (they already were taxed when earned), but benefits above these contributions are fully taxed. Tax laws allow benefits early in retirement to be treated as return of contributions, postponing taxation of benefits until later. Recent estimates indicate that about 80 percent of the benefits typically received are taxable. This taxable ratio, which is equivalent to saying that employees' contributions represent only one-fifth of benefits received, is frequently cited as an indicator of how tough the tax laws are on federal retirees!

At any time during his or her career a federal employee may move into employment that is covered by social security. This can be done before taking on a federal job, during a federal career (moonlighting), or after retirement from the federal career. In 1980 a worker could qualify for the social security minimum benefit after only seven years of covered employment,[31] so the opportunity has certainly existed for federal employees to also qualify for social security. A Social Security Administration study indicated that in 1975 about 40 percent of civil service retirees, or about 443,000 people, received social security as well. An additional 29 percent of CSR annuitants had already qualified for social security but were not yet receiving it. Thus 671,000 people, or 69 percent, would eventually double dip.[32] Many received the minimum of $120 a month. Employee social security contributions usually represent less than 10 percent of the value of the minimum benefit.

A Model Employee Career

The long list of operating characteristics of the salary and pension systems for federal general schedule employees is hard to grasp without a real-life example. I have therefore constructed a "model employee

31. The minimum benefit in social security is an amount in excess of the benefit usually due a retiree. The ordinary benefit is based on (indexed) earnings averaged over up to twenty-six years. When the computation based on this long career yields a social security benefit less than the "minimum benefit," the latter is paid.

32. Daniel N. Price,"Experience of Federal Annuitants under OASDHI: Age and Sex," *Social Security Bulletin*, vol. 42 (July 1979), pp. 33–37.

career" to illustrate some of the features mentioned in this chapter and to entice the reader to read on.

A model career for a professional worker in the federal service might have been as follows. In 1945, at age twenty-five, the employee entered federal service as a GS-5, an entry-level position that paid $2,000 a year at the time. At five- to seven-year intervals for the next thirty years, the employee was promoted, so that in 1974, at age fifty-five, he attained a GS-12 rank. At that time, the annual salary for a GS-12, step 1, was $17,497. The progression up the GS ladder assumed here is consistent with a typical progression through the ranks, according to government estimates.[33]

If the worker had retired at the end of 1974, he would have received an annuity of $9,452 a year. With an expected lifetime of 23.5 years, the present value of this stream of retirement income in 1975 would have been $197,000, about 11 times the earnings in the employee's last year.[34] By contrast, the employee would have contributed a total of $14,000 over his career to the Civil Service Retirement Fund, which if it had earned 6 percent interest a year would have cumulated to about $26,000.

Had the employee continued in the federal service for another five years, until 1979, his salary would have risen from about $18,000 to almost $26,000. Even so, according to the government's wage survey, these salaries were as much as $5,000 below the private sector rates each year. Naturally, the employee would be adding to his civil service retirement credits, so that by 1979 the annuity payable would be up to $15,772. (Such a gain seems impressive for only five years' extra work, even considering the extra $10,000 contributed to the retirement fund.) In fact, had the employee retired at age fifty-five, as originally assumed, the cost-of-living adjustments to the civil service pension would have raised his annuity to $13,912 by 1979. Moreover, if the employee had taken on a new job after retiring from the government in 1975, he might also have qualified for a social security benefit in 1982 (at age sixty-two).

An alternative life pattern illustrates another anomaly of federal

33. Specifically, it is consistent with the estimates used in 1980 by the Board of Actuaries of the Civil Service Retirement System for "Annual Salary Growth before General Schedule Increase." *Board of Actuaries of the Civil Service Retirement System Fifty-Seventh Annual Report,* Committee Print, House Committee on Post Office and Civil Service, 96 Cong. 2 sess. (GPO, 1980), p. 21.

34. Retirement wealth computed on the assumption of a real interest rate (nominal interest less inflation) of 1 percent. This is consistent with the 7 percent interest and 6 percent inflation assumed by the Board of Actuaries of the CSRS. See the discussion in chapter 3.

employment. If the model employee had worked for the federal government only for the first twenty years of his career, through 1964, his civil service retirement income receivable at age sixty-two would have been only $3,548, since it is based on the salary actually received when last employed. If the employee, however, had quit in 1964 but then returned to federal employment from 1978 through 1980, the extra three years of work would have raised the retirement benefit to $11,083, tripling the deferred benefit otherwise receivable!

These examples—based on quite reasonable assumptions and the actual pay and pension provisions of federal employment—illustrate some of the problems to be discussed in subsequent chapters. Pay rates for some occupations are low (and, for others, high) relative to those in the private sector. Retirement benefits may be very high and differ greatly depending on career patterns. Noncoverage of federal employment by social security can lead to excessive retirement benefits. Moreover, these problems interact differently at different stages of a worker's career, affecting the government's ability to retain or attract employees.

Chapter Two

Pay

IT IS IMPORTANT at the outset of the discussion of federal salaries to make clear two of my premises. The first is that with a general schedule work force of about 1.4 million people ranging from lowly clerks to administrators of billion-dollar enterprises, it does not suffice to study only the average salary. Although the key political question may be whether federal salaries are too high or too low, on average, I pass up addressing that question directly in favor of a more disaggregated approach. Indeed, as will be seen, solutions to problems in the federal salary structure that are based on only a single average are almost surely wrongheaded.

The second is that in studying federal salaries and salary-administration practices, it helps to keep in mind how a "normal" labor market operates. One model, dear to economic theorists, is that of perfect competition. Workers are paid the value of their marginal product, and a disequilibrium in the labor market caused by changes in demand or supply is cleared largely by wage-rate changes up or down. These adjustments are made possible because firms and workers have no close bonds to each other; as a result, workers move freely to firms offering a wage advantage and firms compete with one another on that basis. For the most part this model does not seem applicable to private sector labor markets in the United States, and is not at all applicable to federal white-collar markets. Instead, I assume that labor markets are characterized much more by the "career job market." Employers may pay entry-level workers more than the absolute minimum required to maintain employment at the desired levels; workers, in turn, may reach an implicit understanding with their employers that the worker will remain loyal to the firm and will not quit at the first wage advantage observed. The employer, in turn, assures the worker that wages will not be arbitrarily reduced in slack markets and that preference will be shown toward existing workers as opportunities open on a career ladder. These kinds of understandings seem to pervade the nonfarm private sector of the American economy; accordingly, in my analysis of how federal workers (or potential recruits from the private sector) react to salary signals, I assume that the relevant outside world is General Motors, not McDonald's.[1]

Salary Comparisons for the 1970s

During the seventies increases in salaries for federal white-collar workers fell behind those of similar private sector workers, as measured in Bureau of Labor Statistics surveys. According to this source, salary increases amounted to 110 percent for the period 1970–80 for the private white-collar labor force and only 89 percent for federal general schedule workers (table 2-1). Since under federal statute, the 1969 salary levels were supposed to reflect full comparability with the private sector, the subsequent shortfall in federal pay rates would reflect "underpayment" for public employees.[2] By March 1980 BLS data indicate that federal salary rates were 13.5 percent below those in the private sector.

The structure of the shortfall in federal salary rates exhibited considerable differences by occupation and grade level. Table 2-2 shows the level of federal and private salaries at various grades for clerical workers and for professional, administrative, and technical occupations (PAT) in 1980. For PAT occupations in the entry-level grades of GS-5, GS-7, and GS-9, the salary shortfall was 20, 18, and 16 percent, respectively.[3] For grades 9 through 13, the salaries of PAT employees were about 14 percent below those of the private sector; for the two highest grades the shortfall widened again to the 16 to 20 percent range.

Clerical workers' pay was a different story. For the 55 percent of positions in grades 1–4 that were classified as clerical, the BLS data show that federal jobs pay from 11 to 16 percent less than jobs in the private sector. For the most part these are beginners' positions. In the

1. For an excellent discussion of modern labor markets, see Arthur M. Okun, *Prices and Quantities: A Macroeconomic Analysis* (Brookings Institution, 1981), especially chaps. 2 and 3.

2. See the Federal Salary Act of 1967 (5 U.S.C. 5332) for the statutory basis for 1969 pay rates.

3. Up to grade 11 most PAT workers are employed at odd-number grades. They are promoted by two GS levels in that range.

TABLE 2-1. *Rates of Salary Increase in the Private and Public Sectors by Broad Occupational Group, 1971–80*
Percent change

| Date of federal salary increase | Federal | Private[a] | | | Hourly earnings index[c] |
		Total	Clerical	PAT[b]	
January 1971	5.96	6.2	6.2	6.2	6.6
January 1972	5.50	6.6	6.5	6.7	7.2
October 1972	5.14	4.4	4.6	4.1	4.3
October 1973	4.77	5.4	5.4	5.4	5.8
October 1974	5.52	6.4	6.4	6.3	6.8
October 1975	5.00	9.0	9.6	8.3	9.6
October 1976	5.17	7.0	7.3	6.7	6.7
October 1977	7.05	6.9	6.6	7.1	7.6
October 1978	5.50	7.9	7.4	8.3	7.9
October 1979	7.00	7.8	7.8	7.7	8.2
October 1980	9.10	9.1	8.8	9.3	8.6
Cumulative	89.20	109.7	109.5	108.5	114.9
Annual average	6.00	7.1	7.1	7.1	7.3

Sources: Advisory Committee on Federal Pay, *Eight Years of Federal White-Collar Pay Comparability* (ACFP, 1979); "White-Collar Salaries, March 1979," U.S. Department of Labor news release, July 3, 1979; Bureau of Labor Statistics, *National Survey of Professional, Administrative, Technical, and Clerical Pay; March 1972*, Bulletin 1764 (Government Printing Office, 1973); and Bureau of Labor Statistics data.

a. The salary increase for the private sector is for the annual period ending six months before the date of the federal salary increase. This is consistent with the government's current practice of giving October increases based on March data.

b. Professional, administrative, and technical.

c. Includes production and nonsupervisory workers on private nonagricultural payrolls.

more advanced clerical positions in GS levels 5–8, however, the BLS data indicate that federal jobs pay from 1 to 7 percent more than those in the private sector. There are no private sector data for clerical positions above grade 8, but these encompass fewer than 1 percent of all federal clerical jobs.

Three caveats about these data are warranted. First, federal and private sector wages have been compared for the same date, March 1980. But the official government definition of salary comparability is based on equating federal salaries in October to the private sector wage of the preceding March. Wage gains in the private sector between March and October are ignored in the definition of comparability.

Second, it is important to remember that these data refer to *jobs*, not people. An incumbent federal worker who stayed on the job throughout the 1970s would have received salary increases well in excess of the 6.1 percent annual average growth in the general schedule salary rates. At a minimum, five or six step increases would have added about 2 percentage

TABLE 2-2. *Comparison of Private and Federal Salaries by General Schedule Level and Job Category, March 1980*
Dollars unless otherwise specified

GS level	Clerical			Professional, administrative, and technical			Total		
	Private	Federal[a]	Percent difference	Private	Federal[a]	Percent difference	Private	Federal[a]	Percent difference
1	8,110	7,313	10.9	....	7,294	....	8,110	7,309	11.0
2	9,397	8,303	13.2	10,216	8,241	24.0	9,479	8,296	14.3
3	11,130	9,586	16.1	12,132	9,349	29.8	11,254	9,551	17.8
4	12,767	11,201	14.0	12,687	11,033	15.0	12,749	11,149	14.4
5	12,740	12,873	-1.0	15,017	12,503	20.1	13,606	12,733	6.9
6	14,018	14,550	-3.7	14,282	14,245	0.3	14,118	14,419	-2.1
7	15,382	16,215	-5.1	18,512	15,666	17.8	18,107	15,723	15.2
8	17,132	18,335	-6.6	18,454	17,825	3.5	18,208	17,888	1.8
9	n.a.	20,124	n.a.	22,183	19,086	16.2	22,183	19,105	16.1
10	n.a.	22,089	n.a.	n.a.	21,246	n.a.	n.a.	21,259	n.a.
11	n.a.	23,422	n.a.	26,585	23,329	14.0	26,585	23,324	14.0
12	n.a.	27,747	n.a.	31,936	27,949	14.3	31,936	27,947	14.3
13	n.a.	32,077	n.a.	38,278	33,586	14.0	38,278	33,583	14.0
14	n.a.	40,498	n.a.	47,495	39,625	19.9	47,495	39,624	19.9
15	n.a.	42,198	n.a.	53,956	46,727	15.5	53,956	46,724	15.5

Sources: *Comparability of the Federal Statutory Pay Systems with Private Enterprise Pay Rates: Annual Report of the President's Pay Agent, 1980*; and data supplied by the Office of Personnel Management on average GS salary levels and employment by grade and job category.
n.a. Not available.
a. Data include both general schedule and certain other pay systems linked to the general schedule. For total, an "other and unspecified" category was averaged in with the clerical, professional, administrative, and technical groups.

points to the annual wage boost, and any promotions would have also raised pay. Thus the statement that pay for federal positions has fallen below positions in the private sector does not necessarily imply that persons holding federal jobs have fallen behind their contemporaries in the private labor force.

Third, the BLS data on which salary comparisons are made can be challenged on several grounds. Although the survey estimates of salary increases do not seem out of line with other sources of data on earnings changes in the economy (see the last column of table 2-1), at particular grade levels serious questions can be raised about the representativeness of the survey. This problem will be discussed later.

Why Has Federal Pay Fallen Out of Line?

It requires explaining why a system designed to achieve comparability of salaries between public and private sectors has instead resulted in significant shortfalls in federal salaries for professionals and overpayments for clerical workers in advanced jobs. There are two broad reasons for the inability of the system to match pay rates between the sectors—the first having to do with the comparability process itself and the second with deviations from comparability in practice.

The Comparability Process

Even if the comparability process were strictly followed, federal pay rates would be out of line in several respects. As already noted, the federal definition of salary comparability adjusts federal salaries annually each October to equal the private sector rates in March. This is equivalent to building in, on average, a one-year lag in federal pay behind private sector pay.[4] Although this factor might have been ignored in the past, when annual wage increases were small, the one-year lag alone by 1981

4. After the pay increase in October, federal pay would be six months behind the October private sector rate. By the following March, the unchanged federal rate would be one year behind the new March rate for the private sector. Just before the federal raise the following October, federal rates would be one and one-half years behind the private sector. March, being the midpoint of the federal year, represents the average shortfall.

would account for an over 9 percent difference between federal and private pay even if comparability pay increases had been granted.

A second factor within the comparability process that leads to unequal salaries is the averaging of pay rates across occupations at each grade. The BLS survey data for the salaries of sampled jobs at each grade are weighted by federal employment in that job category to produce the average salaries of major occupational groups (clerical, technical, administrative, and professional). These averages are then weighted by federal employment for the major occupational groups in the grade to calculate a private sector average salary for the grade. Only these averages—shown in the total column in table 2-2—are used for the comparability estimates. Since the salaries for different occupations within a grade differ widely in the private sector, equating federal pay to the average private salary in a grade necessarily means that each occupational group in the federal government will be overpaid or underpaid. Thus in table 2-2, if average GS grade 5 salaries were brought up to the average salary in the private sector, clerical pay in the federal government would be about $1,000 above clerical pay in the private sector,[5] while PAT grade 5 salaries in the government would still be about $1,650 below those in the private sector. These differences are even greater when smaller occupational breakdowns are used. See, for example, the data for secretaries and chemists in table 1-5.

A third reason for disparities in pay that would occur even under comparability is that the official procedures smooth the percentage increases at each grade level by making comparisons of points on statistically fitted curves for both the public and private sectors. Since neither sector's curve exactly fits the data points, the comparability salary increase may miss the actual salary averages by a significant amount. This was illustrated in table 1-6, where, for example, the raw data called for a 6.9 percent pay increase at GS-5, while the comparison based on the curves called for an 11.4 percent increase in that grade. These differences do not appear to be random or to even out over the years. As indicated in table 2-3, the pay-line comparison over the years 1977 through 1980 has implied larger pay increases than the raw data for grades 5, 6, 8 (heavily clerical), 13, and 15 in every one of the four

5. The actual GS-5 clerical salary, increased by 6.9 percent (the average shortfall for all GS-5 salaries), gives $13,761, or about $1,000 above the private sector clerical pay rate.

TABLE 2-3. *Comparison of Suggested Average Annual Pay Raises Based on Actual Data and the Comparability Method, by Grade Level, for the Four-Year Period 1977–80*
Percent unless otherwise specified

| GS level | Suggested average annual pay raise | | Number of years column b was more than column a (c) |
	Actual data basis[a] (a)	Comparability basis (b)	
1	10.89	8.37	0
2	11.79	8.15	0
3	14.42	8.54	0
4	11.55	8.36	0
5	3.10	8.26	4
6	− 5.76	8.23	4
7	11.66	8.27	0
8	− 1.50	8.29	4
9	13.72	8.59	0
10	. . .	8.86	. . .
11	12.65	9.21	0
12	9.88	10.14	3
13	9.90	11.38	4
14	14.26	12.95	0
15	10.35	14.87	4

Sources: Annual Office of Personnel Management worksheets.
a. As measured by the annual PATC (professional, administrative, technical, and clerical) survey of the private sector and the March PATCO (professional, administrative, technical, clerical, and other) survey of the general schedule employment.

comparability comparisons. The pay-line raise was lower than the actual data for grades 1–4 and 7, 9, 11, and 14 in each year. A particularly troublesome aspect of the curve comparisons is the size of the difference at grade 15. In the 1980 pay comparison, the data indicated a pay increase of 14.5 percent, while the pay-line comparison indicated 20.9 percent, a difference of about $3,000 at the GS-15 salary level (table 1-6). Because of the way the curves are constructed, very small differences in parameter estimates of the curves can produce large changes in the comparability pay increase that may deviate from the underlying average data, especially at the high grade levels.[6] There is reason, therefore, to be wary of the statistically estimated measures of salary comparability at these higher grades.

6. The pay-line curve for both public and private sectors takes the form $W = ab^i c^{i^2}$ as explained in note 16 of chapter 1. Thus the comparability *percent increase* at any

Deviations from Comparability

Pay comparability as required under the law did not determine pay in the latter part of the 1970s. Except for the October 1976 pay raise, all the increases in general schedule pay have been uniform percentage increases across all grades (see table 1-7). In 1977 the increase of 7.05 percent was based on the average pay increase identified in the comparability calculations,[7] but in the three following years the percentage increase was arbitrarily determined by the president, who used the statutory provision enabling him to offer an "alternative plan." The increases of 5.5 and 7.0 percent in 1978 and 1979, both below the comparability average, were defended as part of the voluntary incomes policy of the Carter administration, whereas the 9.1 percent increase (also below the comparability average) of 1980 appears to have been a preelection sweetener.[8] It should be noted that when an administration abandons comparability as its standard, uniform increases become virtually inevitable—anything else would be lambasted as discriminatory.

In any event, these uniform percentage increases, coupled with a clear tendency for PAT wage increases to exceed clerical wage increases in the private sector after 1976 (table 2-1), produced the imbalances in salaries now observed. The large private sector pay increases in upper-grade-matched jobs (mostly PAT occupations) far outran the hold-down pay increases in the federal pay rates, producing the 14 to 23 percent shortfalls in grades 11–15. The differential growth in private sector occupational pay meant that the uniform pay increases for federal

grade index i is equal to $W^* = AB^iC^{i^2} - 1$, where A, B, and C are the ratios of the parameter estimates from each sector's equation. At grade 15 the index $i = 19$ (see note 16 in chapter 1). This means that if the ratio C rises by 0.1 percent, the pay comparability increase for grade 15 will increase by over 43 percent! (For grade 15, $i = 19$; therefore, $i^2 = 361$. If the C term in the equation rises by 0.1 percent, the value of W^* will be $(1.001)^{361} = 1.435$ of its former value.) Although the comparability curves seem to fit the data fairly precisely, an error of 0.1 percent in a point estimate of a coefficient such as C in, say, the private sector equation cannot be ruled out.

7. The percent increase in each grade is weighted by aggregate salaries to arrive at the average. This procedure gives greater weight to comparability pay increases in the upper grades than if employment weights were used.

8. President Carter's initial estimate for the October 1980 pay raise was 6.2 percent. See *The Budget of the United States Government, Fiscal Year 1981*, p. 311.

workers were more than adequate in the advanced clerical positions in grades 5–8, but inadequate for the entry-level professional positions.

Unless salaries for clerical positions rise relative to PAT positions in the private sector, there is no way that uniform percentage increases for federal workers can realign current pay imbalances. If President Carter had not held down average federal salary boosts in the late 1970s, the shortfall in pay for PAT workers would have been less, but only at the cost of even greater overpayment in federal clerical positions. President Reagan's plan to severely limit federal pay should help to keep clerical positions more in line with those in the private sector, but only at the cost of a worsening shortfall for PAT workers at all levels.

An additional salary imbalance exists at the grade 15 level and for the Senior Executive Service managerial positions just above the general schedule. According to the Executive Salary Cost-of-Living Adjustment Act executive salaries are supposed to be raised each year by the average increase for the general schedule rates of pay.[9] Thus executive pay increases for 1977 through 1980 should have cumulated to 31.8 percent; instead they amounted to 5.5 percent, as Congress repeatedly failed to adjust its own salary and held high executive-branch officials to the same austere diet.[10] The pay rate for officials at the executive level V is the statutory ceiling for general schedule salaries. Since this ceiling rose only from $47,500 to $50,113 in the 1977–80 period, while pay for GS-15s was rising by 31.8 percent, the ceiling in 1981 determined pay for about two-thirds of the people in grade 15. (In the fall of 1981 almost all of grade 15 and part of grade 14 were paid at the ceiling.)

Similarly, the Senior Executive Service is limited by law to a basic salary no higher than that of level IV in the executive schedule. That level was increased only once (from $50,000 to $52,750 in 1979) in the years between 1977 and 1980. Moreover, the former supergrade employees, who converted to Senior Executive Service status in 1979, were held to the ceiling that previously applied to their positions. For almost all the Senior Executive Service, that ceiling was $50,113 until 1982.

The upshot of these restrictions was that at the top of the general schedule and in the Senior Executive Service, pay rates were dominated by a single-ceiling provision. As a result, in 1980, 33,500 people received

9. 89 Stat. 419.

10. For a discussion of the linkage between executive and congressional pay, see Robert W. Hartman and Arnold R. Weber, eds., *The Rewards of Public Service: Compensating Top Federal Officials* (Brookings Institution, 1980).

the same salary. If the BLS survey data for the private sector are correct, then in 1980 salary rates at the GS-15 level were 14.5 percent too low. Since the Senior Executive Service is made up of people in jobs that supervise the GS-15 workers and lower grades, a properly functioning salary system would provide salaries for these managerial posts perceptibly higher. Thus, for example, since the 1980 BLS survey found that private sector equivalents of GS-15 earned $53,956, Senior Executive Service pay, if made equivalent to private sector pay, might have ranged to up to 25 percent above that salary level. This would have meant an SES pay range of $54,000 to $67,000 (in round numbers) instead of the $50,113 earned by most senior officials in 1980. For these and related reasons the Commission on Executive, Legislative, and Judicial Salaries recommended in December 1980 that the upper limit for SES salaries be set at $76,000.[11] President Carter, initially with the concurrence of President Reagan, recommended that the ceiling for the Senior Executive Service be raised to $61,600 in early 1981 and $65,000 in October 1981.[12] In President Reagan's budget amendments in the spring of 1981, this recommendation was dropped in favor of a continued freeze on Senior Executive Service basic pay. Congress supported this freeze until late 1981.[13]

At the upper reaches of the general schedule, for administrators in grades 13–15 and in the Senior Executive Service, basic salaries can be supplemented by a limited system of merit pay and bonuses. The "merit pay" program for the GS-13–15 levels (begun in 1982) provides that only half of the general schedule pay increase be paid automatically to managers in those grades. The funds saved by paying only half the increase and by eliminating the longevity pay steps for managers are then pooled within each agency and used to provide merit increases up to the maximum salary for GS-15. This merit increase becomes the new base salary for the employee. In the case of career members of the Senior Executive Service, the law permits up to one-half of them to receive a lump-sum bonus payment of as much as 20 percent of base salary. (In practice, in SES's first year of experience, 1980, bonuses were restricted

11. See *Report of the Commission on Executive, Legislative, and Judicial Salaries, December 1980* (GPO, 1980).

12. *Budget of the United States Government, Fiscal Year 1982—Appendix*, pt. 7.

13. In late 1981 the ceilings on salary were raised to $58,500 for the Senior Executive Service and to $57,500 for the general schedule, as a result of the provisions in the Third Continuing Resolution on the Budget for fiscal 1982.

to fewer than 25 percent of the eligible members, because of a threat by Congress to eliminate bonuses altogether.)

These extras to regular salary somewhat ameliorate the shortfall in pay for those employees who receive them,[14] but they create problems of their own. One problem is that with the extreme compression of regular salaries, managers feel a need to use bonuses to reward worker experience and difficulty of job, as well as to provide incentives for inducing an employee to take on greater responsibility or for preventing an employee from quitting. These objectives would ordinarily be handled through promotions and the regular salary benefits that accompany them. But with the pay ceiling it is inevitable that in the Senior Executive Service bonuses will be used for these objectives, even though the intent of the law was that they should be a reward for particularly adept service over the year being evaluated. Thus in 1980, 30 percent of the SES bonuses (and rank awards) were granted to SES members in the top two levels, which contain 16 percent of the SES population, while 11 percent of the awards went to the lowest three levels in the SES, which contain 20 percent of the SES population.[15] The result of subjecting managers to crosscurrents of objectives in distributing bonuses is that the system becomes subject to confusion, charges of favoritism, and decline of morale.[16]

How Does the System Respond to Imbalance?

Survey data indicate that federal jobs in the PAT occupations are underpaid significantly relative to matched jobs in the private sector, while some clerical positions in government are somewhat underpaid

14. In October 1980 eight agencies put merit pay plans into effect for GS-13–15 employees. The average pay increase for the managers in the program was about 12 percent, but some managers received as much as a 24 percent increase. Except in two small agencies (Commission on Civil Rights and Farm Credit Administration) few managers failed to get the 9.1 percent increase that was the general schedule increase. See Efstathia A. Siegel, "Eight Agencies Link Pay to Performance: Will Merit Pay Work?" *Management* (Spring 1981), pp. 15–17.

15. See *Senior Executive Service*, Hearings before the Subcommittee on Civil Service of the House Committee on Post Office and Civil Service, 97 Cong. 1 sess. (Government Printing Office, 1981), p. 20.

16. See General Accounting Office, *Actions Needed to Enhance the Credibility of Senior Executive Service Performance Award Programs*, Report FPCD 81-65 (GPO, 1981); and William J. Lanouette, "SES—From Civil Service Showpiece to Incipient Failure in Two Years," *National Journal*, July 18, 1981, p. 1296.

TABLE 2-4. *Change in General Schedule Full-Time Employment between March 1977 and March 1980, by Grade and Occupation*

| | Clerical | | | | Professional, administrative, and technical | | | |
| | Employment | | Change | | Employment | | Change | |
GS level	1977	1980	Number	Percent	1977	1980	Number	Percent
1	1,792	1,542	−250	−14.0	278	286	8	2.9
2	20,943	18,517	−2,426	−11.6	3,328	2,085	−1,243	−37.3
3	84,389	73,852	−10,537	−12.5	12,847	10,185	−2,662	−20.7
4	131,583	122,358	−9,225	−7.0	35,522	35,445	−77	−0.2
5	113,046	107,285	−5,761	−5.1	58,632	63,556	4,924	8.4
6	53,024	49,689	−3,335	−6.3	28,841	32,019	3,178	11.0
7	15,109	16,326	1,217	8.1	109,019	110,039	948	0.9
8	4,173	4,296	123	2.9	22,069	21,192	−877	−4.0
9	2,150	2,097	−53	−2.5	131,870	132,750	880	−0.7
10	439	473	34	7.7	24,695	27,735	3,040	11.0
11	277	246	−31	−11.2	146,750	152,419	5,669	3.9
12	91	66	−25	−27.5	141,920	158,049	16,129	11.4
13	25	26	1	4.0	105,680	110,180	4,500	4.3
14	4	6	2	50.0	51,336	57,582	6,037	11.8
15	5	4	−1	−20.0	24,651	27,582	2,931	11.9
Total	427,058	396,785	−30,273	−7.1	897,510	940,895	43,385	4.8

Sources: Civil Service Commission, Bureau of Manpower Information Systems, "March 1977 PATCO Survey"; and Office of Personnel Management, "March 1979 PATCO Report Totals," and "January 1980 PATCO Report Totals."

and others somewhat overpaid. How does the government respond to these imbalances?

If one assumes, first, that private sector relative wage rates accurately measure the relative productivity of clerical versus PAT workers in both private and federal sectors, one would predict that the demand by the federal government for PAT workers would rise relative to the demand for clerical workers. For example, if PAT wages are $15 an hour and clerical wages are $5 an hour in the private sector—and the productivity relation is also 3:1—whereas the federal government offers PAT workers $10 an hour and clerical workers $7.50 an hour, it makes sense for a federal manager to fire (or not hire) four clerical workers and hire three professional workers for the same total salary. The three professionals would raise output by 9 units; the forgone clericals would reduce output by only 4 units.

It is at least mildly encouraging that some of this kind of change appears to be happening in federal employment. Table 2-4 shows that employment of clerical workers between 1977 and 1980 dropped by about 7 percent, while employment in PAT job titles rose by about 5 percent. Moreover, since the government rarely dismisses workers, one would expect to see the job reductions among clerical workers concentrated in entry-level positions, where turnover is highest and where reductions in employment can be made by simply not replacing people who leave. This, too, is borne out by the data, which show that the greatest reduction in filled clerical job slots occurred at grades 3 and 4, mainly beginners' positions.

Although it is comforting that the government is economizing on the most overpaid group, this simple analysis leaves out the institutional constraints on federal managers' behavior, nor can it explain the pattern of employment growth in the PAT categories. To find out what the response of the bureaucracy to wage imbalances between the federal and private sectors really is, some of this detail needs to be supplied.

Institutional Constraints

Federal agencies are limited in personnel decisions by two primary constraints. One of these is the allocation of a limited number of slots, or permanent positions. Ordinarily these slot limits are determined as part of the budget process. Until 1981 the slot limit was changed annually and was based on the number of permanent positions as of September

30, the last day of the fiscal year. In 1978 the Civil Service Reform Act set a personnel ceiling for the entire government, and in 1981 agencies were given ceilings in terms of full-time equivalent positions for an entire year. Although there are strict controls over the number of positions, there is no comparable limitation on the grade structure of the work force. Data on the grade structure are collected and reported by the agency to the Office of Personnel Management and to the Office of Management and Budget, but little in the way of strict guidance is issued.[17] New positions and grades are treated in an ad hoc fashion.

The second limit on agency personnel is the budget. Funds for paying salaries and fringe benefit charges against agencies are provided in appropriations lines called "salaries and expenses."[18] These appropriations also provide funds for travel by agency personnel, moving expenses, rental and utility charges incurred, purchase of office equipment, and computer and consultant services and the like. To a large extent agencies are free to shift money from one object to another within the salary and expense budget.

Because of this system of control over agency employment, the constraint over the number of positions nearly always dominates the budget constraint. What subagency managers fight for is the allocation of more slots for their office; the money can always be found, if necessary by the transfer of funds originally targeted for travel or typewriters or the like. But when a subagency has completed its hiring up to the personnel ceiling, even low-priority spending for travel and equipment cannot be diverted to personnel, even if it would have a higher payoff there.[19]

The system in place gives a significant incentive for government agencies to hire more high-grade employees relative to low-grade employees than their relative wages would warrant. Managers can ignore the payroll cost and just worry about staying under the personnel ceiling. As long as the productivity of a high-grade worker exceeds that of a low-grade one, it makes sense for the agency head to hire him or her. This factor alone could explain why, as clerical vacancies open, agencies are inclined to restore their slot quota by hiring professionals. It also could

17. An exception is the SES, whose positions are allocated to the agencies.
18. Sometimes the appropriations that fund salaries are called "departmental management" or "limitation on administrative expenses." For a full listing of such accounts, see *Budget of the United States Government, Fiscal Year 1982—Appendix*, pt. 3.
19. Appendix A formalizes some of the personnel implications of the dual-constraint system.

explain part of the upward drift in grades within the clerical and PAT occupations (table 2-4).[20] In short, although pay differences between high-grade and low-grade employees are much smaller in federal jobs than in the private sector, the greater relative growth of employment in high-grade jobs is probably more the result of personnel constraints than of relative wage rates.

Pattern of Employment Growth

Much of this discussion relates to what the government as employer wants to do, but not to the willingness of labor to do it. As noted earlier, the BLS data indicate a wide underpayment for federal PAT occupations in the entry-level grades. How does the government manage to recruit people if this is true?

One answer is that government managers use the only sweetener available to them: they promise recruits rapid promotions. Since a promotion to a higher grade increases pay by about 20 percent (see table 2-2, PAT occupations in odd-numbered grades), a job applicant, expecting significant future raises, may be willing to enter government service at a lower wage than he or she could command elsewhere.

The employment data for PAT workers is consistent with this hypothesis. Table 2-4 shows that although employment remained fairly constant in grades 5–9, which are entry-level or low-experience grades for professional and managerial workers, it rose sharply from grades 11 through 14, the grades to which the entrants would be promoted. The data could reflect new hires from the private sector, rather than promotions from within; it seems likely, however, that the data mainly reflect promotions.

For an agency to fulfill its promise of promoting entrants that are hired at below-market salaries, it must justify creating a new position at the higher grade. It does this by writing a job description for the position to be upgraded that details the responsibilities of the position. While often the federal employee is given greater responsibilities to warrant his promotion, sometimes the job description is inflated to overstate the job's importance. Many studies of position grading in the federal government have been made. The most recent was a study of over 800 general schedule positions in twenty-one federal agencies made by the Civil Service Commission in 1978. The results, summarized in table 2-5,

20. It also explains the anecdotes about federal employees earning $40,000 who type their own memoranda or laboriously copy statistics.

TABLE 2-5. *Results of Classification Audits Conducted by the Civil Service Commission, by Grade Range, 1976–78*
Percent unless otherwise specified

GS grade range	Number of positions audited	Classification[a]		
		Over- graded	Under- graded	Correct
1–4	168	10.1	4.8	82.1
5–9	359	12.3	4.7	76.9
10–12	210	6.2	1.4	88.1
13–15	116	20.7	0.0	73.3
Total	853	11.5	3.3	80.2

Source: Civil Service Commission, Bureau of Personnel Management Evaluation, "A Report on Study of Position Classification Accuracy in Executive Branch Occupations under the General Schedule" (July 1978), attachment I.
a. Figures do not sum to 100 percent because the category "number series/title error" (about 5 percent of the sample) is omitted.

show that about 11.5 percent of the positions were overgraded and 3.3 percent were undergraded. The rate of overgrading was by far the greatest in the GS-13–15 range, consisting almost exclusively of professional and managerial jobs. In the study the evaluators were asked to determine the causes of misclassification. "The most frequently cited cause for the overgrading of positions was agency management considerations . . . a broad category of management influence on the classification process. An example is management pressure on a classifier."[21] This kind of pressure is what one would expect from a supervisor who has promised a recruit a promotion and needs to fulfill the promise. While some job overclassification is probably done to make up for underpayment of federal workers, it would be wrong to claim that such overclassification is universal. Even with all the pressures, the study shows that 80 percent of the general schedule jobs are properly graded or undergraded. Nevertheless, the overgrading of the other 20 percent can lead to some absurdities.[22]

An alternative course for a federal manager to take when unable to pay the market wage for a new recruit is to reduce the acceptable

21. Civil Service Commission, Bureau of Personnel Management Evaluation, "A Report on Study of Position Classification Accuracy in Executive Branch Occupations under the General Schedule" (July 1978), p. 9.
22. For an extreme example of an overgraded job description, see Bernard H. Baum, "The Upward Pressures on Position Classification," in Frank J. Thompson, ed., *Classics of Public Personnel Policy* (Oak Park, Ill.: Moore Publishing Company, 1979), pp. 24–25.

qualifications for the job.[23] This is often the manager's only alternative, because the applicants for the job at the below-market wage offered are likely to have lower credentials than the applicants for an equivalent but higher-paying private sector job. This way of managing the failure of federal entry-level wages to compete with the private sector has potentially grave implications for the future performance of the federal work force. If federal agencies are taking in less qualified people at the entry level, the pool of highly qualified people available for promotion to higher levels of responsibility will decrease, and after some years' time there will be a general diminution of quality and competence throughout the work force. Unfortunately, it is next to impossible to prove that such reduced standards are evolving, for little hard data on productivity and performance in government jobs exist.

I have stressed the reaction of agency managers to imbalances in wage rates at entry-level grades because it is at those levels that most employment adjustments are made. At higher grade levels imbalances are simply lived with, though in different ways. For the advanced clerical jobs, the above-market government salaries constitute a "rent," an unearned increment, to the positions' occupants. When vacancies arise, agency managers have the luxury of being able to choose from a long queue of applicants. Very often this means that the agency can hire unusually well qualified people and can satisfy affirmative action and other goals as well.

For the advanced professional and managerial posts the effect of below-market salaries is not as great as at the entry level. There is pressure for grade promotions in this range as well, but because of pay ceilings they do not guarantee much of a pay raise. But employees do not quit—turnover is small—for good reason. As discussed in the next chapter, the federal retirement program is designed to make quitting costly for an employee with ten or more years of service. As a result, most employees in upper-level positions simply stay until they are eligible for retirement. A small proportion of the underpaid high-level professionals do leave before becoming eligible for retirement; all indications are that these workers are the most competent ones, who

23. It is interesting to note the similarities in the government's response to wage imbalance with that of universities seeking to maintain a single faculty salary across specialties. See Richard B. Freeman, "Demand for Labor in a Non-Profit Market: University Faculty," in Daniel S. Hamersmesh, ed., *Labor in the Public and Non-Profit Sectors* (Princeton University Press, 1975), especially pp. 103–09.

can attract offers from the private sector sufficiently lucrative to make them give up substantial retirement plan investments. Once eligibility for retirement is reached, employees retire at overwhelmingly high rates. In the year ending March 1980, 37 percent of those eligible to retire did so; among those eligible whose pay was at the ceiling, retirements ran at the rate of 57 percent.[24] Among newly eligible top bureaucrats aged fifty-five through fifty-nine, 75 percent retired in 1980.[25] If these retirement rates should continue, it would accelerate promotion rates from lower ranks of the general schedule work force. The upshot of these forces is that underpayment of PAT occupations in the federal work force leads to (a) the overgrading of positions, (b) abnormally rapid promotions, and (c) a situation in which relatively less qualified people fill the available slots—first at the bottom of the PAT grades, but eventually at all levels.

Is Pay Comparability the Right Goal?

The preceding discussion assumes that comparability of salary between the public and private sectors is a desirable standard for setting federal pay. By paying the same wage as in a comparable private job, the federal government would be able to attract and retain personnel without paying an unnecessary bonus or exacting an unfair penalty on its workers. Moreover, insofar as private sector relative wages reflect relative productivity of different workers, a federal salary structure based on such differences would accurately reflect the opportunity cost of luring employees into federal jobs. There are two broad challenges to this fundamental rationale for pay comparability.

The first is that "salaries" and "jobs" inadequately describe the relevant considerations in a functioning labor market. Both employer and employee should be and are concerned with other pecuniary emoluments—such as insurance and retirement benefits. This point is certainly well taken, and in the next chapter I deal with retirement pay, the largest nonsalary benefit. A more difficult qualification to deal with is the possibility of systematic differences between sectors in nonpecuniary job conditions. If federal jobs, for example, are more satisfying, stimulating, and secure (or whatever other attributes are valued by workers)

24. Data cited by Clifford I. Gould, Director, Federal Personnel and Compensation Division, General Accounting Office, in *Senior Executive Service*, Hearings, p. 25.

25. Ibid. See also Lanouette, "SES—From Civil Service Showpiece to Incipient Failure," p. 1296.

than private sector jobs, the fact that pay (or total compensation) is lower in the federal sector will produce no adverse effects on federal recruitment or retention. In such a case the pay differential is simply a tax the federal worker willingly pays to have a job he views as better.

While compensating differentials are an important qualification to mechanical application of the comparability standard, in practice it is hard to make a systematic statement about their importance in federal-private comparisons. For high-powered jobs at the very top of the government, the power and prestige of the positions are unquestionably without parallel in the private sector. And federal employment in jobs comparable to blue-collar occupations is probably more secure than in the private sector (many Postal Service jobs, for example, would fall into this category). But for the bulk of the white-collar occupations that are the subject of this study, there is no systematic evidence on job conditions. Federal workers give up the right to strike, and their jobs (recently, at least) seem to confer little prestige, but they are less likely to be dismissed and have vast job-grievance protections. Some positions in the federal sector are enormously rewarding (astronaut), others may be dangerous (foreign service), and the bulk are probably just like private sector jobs. Thus, although the government pay should probably be made flexible enough to take advantage of favorable working conditions in some jobs and to make up for unfavorable conditions in others, it is hard to draw any rule for overall pay-setting based on differences in intersectoral job conditions.

The second objection to comparability is even more fundamental. The doctrine of "comparable worth," offered most prominently by some labor unions and women's groups, contends that the market system is a biased foundation on which to base wages, owing to a long history of wage discrimination against certain jobs with high concentrations of women and minority workers. They charge discrimination when plumbers, painters, and laboratory technicians are paid substantially more than those in jobs requiring equivalent experience and skill, such as librarians, executive secretaries, and nurses. Instead of comparability they recommend setting pay based on an objective rating system to determine the value of the job to the organization. At least to some extent the current general schedule grading system implicitly accepts a nonmarket-based system of determining the equivalence of jobs. For instance, when repeated labor market surveys show that clerical positions in the GS-5–8 range are paid less than other occupations in the same grade, the government does not conclude that the clerical positions are "overgraded." Indeed, the classification system continues to treat all GS-5 jobs as equivalent and, in effect, compensates for "discrimination" in the private sector by counting PAT wages along with clerical wages in determining the average private sector wage in the grade.

It would be oversimplistic to suggest that the status quo in federal wages, with higher than comparable wages for advanced clerical workers and uncompetitive wages for entry-level professionals, is a desirable implementation of comparable worth considerations. Underpayment in the lower PAT positions impose the costs of quality erosion in the work force and overgrading of some positions. The only costs of maintaining higher than comparable wages for federal clerical workers are fiscal. A possible solution that involves splitting the GS into separate occupational groups is discussed in chapter 4.

Comparable worth is a legitimate area of debate for those concerned about the past and future status of female workers on the one hand and taxpayers on the other. But simple, back door solutions that lower the quality of the entire civil service should not be sought. Indeed the approach of separating the discrimination issue from general civil service pay is consistent with the actions of labor unions that attempt to address wage imbalances by increasing wages in female-dominated positions, never by lowering wages in other positions.[26]

Consistency with Human Capital Studies

A number of studies of federal employee salaries reached the conclusion that federal workers are overpaid. These studies did not assess whether particular *jobs* are better paid in the federal or private sectors, but rather whether *people* with equal human capital characteristics, such as education and experience, earn different amounts in the two sectors. Invariably these studies show that when human capital characteristics (and other characteristics like race, sex, and residence) are statistically

26. The idea of comparable worth has been gaining some momentum. In the summer of 1981 Local 101 of the American Federation of State, County, and Municipal Employees staged a largely successful strike against the city of San Jose, California, over the issue and won $1.4 million in bonuses to workers in low-paid female-dominated jobs. Attempts to compare wages and "worth" of dissimilar jobs in Equal Pay Act and Civil Rights Act discrimination cases have been argued in court. The Supreme Court ruling in *County of Washington (Oregon)* v. *Gunther* was ambiguous but encouraging to comparable worth supporters. See John H. Bunzel, "To Each According to Her Worth?" *Public Interest,* no. 67 (Spring 1982), pp. 77–93.

FIGURE 2-1. *Interaction of Salaries with Human Capital and Job Levels in the Public and Private Sectors*

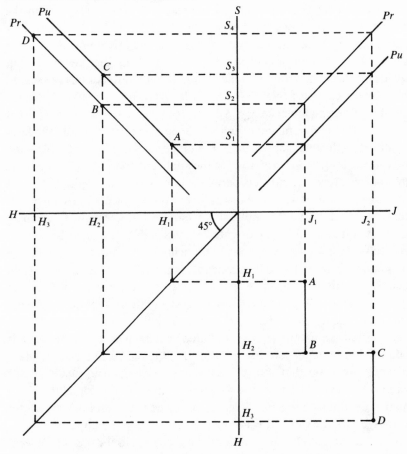

Note: S = salaries; J = job levels; H = human capital; Pu = public sector; Pr = private sector.

controlled, federal workers are paid higher salaries than people in the private sector.[27]

Is this finding consistent with the fact that jobs in the federal government are paid less than comparable jobs in the private sector? The answer is yes, and it can be illustrated as follows. In figure 2-1 the upper-right quadrant shows salaries (S) offered in the public and private sectors

27. The main studies reaching these conclusions are Sharon P. Smith, *Equal Pay in the Public Sector: Fact or Fantasy* (Princeton University Industrial Relations Section, 1977), and Joseph F. Quinn, "Pay Differentials among Mature Workers in the Public and Private Sectors," Discussion Paper 445-77 (University of Wisconsin—Madison, Institute for Research on Poverty, October 1977).

for equivalent jobs (J) with the more responsible jobs requiring greater training, experience, and so on, being at the right of the diagram. By assumption, for any level of J, S is greater in the private than in the public sector as shown on the lines labeled Pr and Pu. Now consider what happens when the federal government and private firms compete for workers for a particular job, J_1. The vertical lines in the lower-right quadrant show the array of human capital characteristics (H) possessed by job applicants for two illustrative J levels. Since the federal government is offering a lower salary (S_1) than the private sector (S_2) for jobs at the J_1 level, the federal government will be able to attract only the less-qualified applicants (shown at point A in the second quadrant), while the private sector gets the cream (B) of the applicant pool. Thus for the same job the private sector attracts people with more human capital (H_2) than the public sector (H_1) does. One would then observe (upper-left quadrant) that at low-salary, S_1, the public sector employs people with H_1 in human capital (point A), while the private sector's high S_2 attracts people with H_2 (point B), both for a J_1 level job. For a higher-skilled job, J_2, the array of human capital supplied by applicants is greater (line CD in lower-right quadrant), but once again the public sector's inferior salary will attract the less qualified applicants (C), while the private sector will draw from the top of the applicant pool (D). If the public sector salary (S_3) for job J_2 is plotted against the H_2 level of human capital it attracts, the result is point C in the upper-left quadrant (point D is the private sector salary for a J_2 level job that attracts H_3 human capital). The result of this exercise is that the salary line for public employees will at all levels of human capital (see upper-left quadrant) lie above that of private sector employees (AC extended is above DB extended in the upper-left quadrant). Thus relatively low salaries for a given job in the federal government are consistent with the fact that the government pays more than the private sector to people with given human capital attributes. The key is that the federal government is placing people with given human capital in more responsible and demanding positions than the private sector is.[28]

I want to be quick to point out that the discussion here simply demonstrates that it is possible for federal jobs to be underpaid at the

---

28. If the reader thinks this is implausible, consider two common pieces of anecdotal evidence. One is the whiz kid, aged twenty-eight (low human capital and experience), who is senior adviser to the president and earns $50,000 a year. The other is the young lawyer who willingly takes a low-paying federal job because she knows she could never get such a responsible position in private practice until she was much older.

same time that federal workers of a given characteristic earn more than their private sector counterparts. Other patterns of response of human capital characteristics to salary differences between the two sectors will produce different results.[29] But when that possibility is considered along with the pressures for rapid promotion when federal salaries are too low, it is not surprising to find that federal salaries are higher than private ones for a given human capital embodied in a worker. The human capital studies simply do not supply any evidence on the degree to which pay for a given job is too high or too low in the federal government.

What those studies do indicate, however, is that one should not be sanguine about low salaries for federal jobs. One interpretation of the situation I have been discussing is that the federal government takes a given amount of human capital and places it in more responsible jobs than the private sector does—a boon for efficiency through public employment! A more correct interpretation is that low salaries force the federal government to lower quality (of people) standards for a given job and then give incentives for jobs to be overgraded, so as to make up initial salary shortfalls by promotions. This second interpretation means that a problem of overpayment (and of quality) exists in the federal work force, but it is not one that can be solved by lowering salaries.

This demonstration that my finding of too low salaries in most federal PAT jobs is compatible with other findings that human capital is better rewarded in federal jobs is actually overkill with regard to the human capital studies. Those studies almost always find the really significant "rents" going to female federal workers. Those rents may simply be a reflection of the excess pay for clerical workers in higher grades evident in the BLS data.[30] Moreover, the data used in the human capital studies have for the most part included blue-collar and Postal Service positions. For reasons having nothing to do with the white-collar pay system, federal jobs in both these areas do seem to be overrewarded compared

29. For example, if in the figure the gap between the human capital levels of hires for any given job is narrower (A and B, for example, in the lower-right quadrant are closer together), then the federal wage line would not lie above the private wage line in the upper-left quadrant. Pure human capitalists, who think that human capital variables embody all productivity differences and that jobs *require* a fixed amount of H, would argue for A and B being a single point. For discussion, see Lester C. Thurow, *Investments in Human Capital* (Wadsworth, 1970).

30. The latest data used by Smith, *Equal Pay in the Public Sector*, were for 1975. In that period, before the hold-down of federal wages, the overpayment of federal clerical workers probably extended even into the lower grades.

with private sector jobs. Thus, insofar as the high observed salaries for federal workers compared with those for private sector workers of equal education and experience are due to these other pay systems, they have no bearing on whether white-collar pay is out of line.

In a recent empirical study, George Borjas demonstrates that federal agencies seem to reward differentially a given amount of human capital.[31] After controlling for education, experience, race, sex, region, health, and military service, Borjas found that the Transportation and Justice departments paid employees about $3,000 more in 1977 than the Veterans Administration and the Agriculture Department.[32] He attributes these differences to the political importance of the agency, its constituency strength, and the internal cohesion of the bureaucracy in the agency. These factors mean that "not only is the civil service pay structure far from an inflexible collection of rules and regulations, it is actually administered in a manner suggested by the political theory . . . [constituencies, cohesion] of federal wage policy."[33] The implication is that promotions and job classifications are manipulated to a greater or lesser extent by agencies and that this produces the pay variation among agencies.

There is, however, a much simpler explanation for Borjas's interagency findings than political manipulation. The two high-paying federal agencies (after controlling for human capital and demographics), according to Borjas, are the Transportation and Justice departments. In 1980, 42 percent of the full-time white-collar labor force of the Transportation Department was in the category "air traffic control"; 21 percent of the Justice Department work force was classified in "criminal investigating."[34] Both air traffic controllers and FBI men are highly paid relative to their age and formal education because of the large amount of on-the-job training and the health hazards of their jobs.

At the other end of the spectrum, the Veterans Administration and Agriculture Department are low payers, according to Borjas's data.

31. George J. Borjas, *Wage Policy in the Federal Bureaucracy* (American Enterprise Institute for Public Policy Research, 1980).
32. These are the greatest variations Borjas finds among the largest federal agencies. I omitted the Postal Service for reasons given above.
33. Borjas, *Wage Policy*, p. 46.
34. The Justice Department is also a heavy user of lawyers, employing 23 percent of all federal "general attorneys," while hiring only 2.6 percent of the total work force. Lawyers, in both private and public sectors, are highly paid given their education and training.

Thirty-five percent of the VA labor force are nurses and nursing assistants. These jobs are chronically underpaid in both public and private sectors. The Agriculture Department's salary scale is pulled down by a large number of technical workers in biological science occupations (22 percent of the department's work force, of which over half are forestry technicians), whose median pay was $6,800 below that of the average federal worker. Their salaries appear to be low in part because the federal government employs about one-third of all such people (limited private sector opportunities), and in part because of an oversupply of such workers (perhaps due to the attractions of outdoor work in the environmental field).[35] In any event, with these large occupational differences between departments, it would seem unnecessary to resort to theorizing about political influence in accounting for most of the interagency differences in salary.[36]

Some Qualms about the BLS Data

All analyses of federal salaries for particular jobs in relation to comparable ones in the private sector must use data from the Bureau of Labor Statistics survey. They are the only such data for matched jobs available. However, several characteristics of the BLS survey and its uses warrant caution about drawing firm conclusions.

The Bureau of Labor Statistics each year defines a minimum size of firm to sample, currently ranging from 50 to 250 employees, depending on industry. This defines the "scope of survey." The bureau then studies the employment and salary records of about 10 percent of the firms within the scope of the survey, which employ about one-third of all the workers in the scope. Salaries for each occupation and work level are obtained from this sample and are weighted in a way that reflects the probability of a firm being selected for the sample.[37]

Table 2-6 illustrates the sampling outcomes for GS-14 equivalent jobs in the private sector survey of March 1981. The number of positions

35. See Bureau of Labor Statistics, *Occupational Outlook Handbook, 1980–81 Edition,* Bulletin 2075 (GPO, 1980), pp. 276–78.
36. All data in this section are from Office of Personnel Management, *Occupations of Federal White-Collar Workers, October 31, 1980* (GPO, 1980).
37. A full description of the methodology is given in Bureau of Labor Statistics, *National Survey of Professional, Administrative, Technical, and Clerical Pay, March 1981,* Bulletin 2108 (GPO, 1981), app. A.

TABLE 2-6. *Size of the Bureau of Labor Statistics Sample and Dispersion of Salaries for GS-14, 1981*

	Employees		
Occupation	Number in scope of survey	Estimated number surveyed[a]	Dispersion of salaries (percent)[b]
Professional			
Attorney V	1,587	510	22.4
Chemist VII	1,622	570	13.7
Chief accountant IV	163	55	7.8
Engineer VII	14,450	5,200	17.3
Administrative			
Personnel director IV	352	115	26.6

Source: Bureau of Labor Statistics, *National Survey of Professional, Administrative, Technical, and Clerical Pay, March 1981*, Bulletin 2108 (GPO, 1981), pp. 11, 29, 34.

a. Estimated by applying the average of the ratios of workers surveyed to workers in the universe by industry, weighted by employment in the industry for each occupation to the number reported in the sample universe.

b. Difference between salary at third quartile and first quartile divided by median salary.

whose salaries were actually studied in the sample ranges from over 5,000 for the engineer job level down to 55 for the accountant level. The observed salaries for these jobs are not tightly bunched at a single level; for three of the five jobs surveyed that are GS-14 equivalents, the dispersion around the median salary is about 20 percent. For personnel directors, for example, the median salary in 1981 was $53,700, but 25 percent of the people received more than $61,500 and 25 percent were paid less than $47,135. One implication of this dispersion is that no one should get excited when the BLS survey shows that federal workers' salaries are 5 percent over or under those in the private sector. A federal worker making 5 percent less than the median private sector wage would still be earning more than almost 40 percent of his private sector counterparts if the dispersion around the median is 20 percent. On the other hand, when federal pay falls to 20 percent below the median, the federal worker would be making less than about 85 percent of his private sector equivalents.

The bureau computes an average salary for each sampled job title. It reports that the sampling error of these average salaries—the likelihood that the estimate deviates from the true average in the survey scope—is tolerably small. Thus, for example, if the estimated mean salary for a particular job is $50,000, the probability that the true mean lies outside the range $47,000 to $53,000 is under 10 percent.[38] So far so good.

38. Ibid., p. 33.

TABLE 2-7. *Representativeness of the Sampled Occupations for GS-14 in the Bureau of Labor Statistics Survey, 1981*

Occupation	Federal jobs in occupation	Federal jobs in major occupational group	Coverage of sampled occupation (percent)
Professional			
Attorney V	3,399	. . .	. . .
Chemist VII	803	. . .	. . .
Chief accountant IV	609	. . .	. . .
Engineer VII	10,423	. . .	. . .
Total	15,234	28,544	53.4
Administrative			
Personnel director IV	322	. . .	. . .
Total	322	30,204	1.1
All occupations	15,556	58,748	26.5

Source: *Annual Report of the President's Pay Agent, 1981*, p. 17.

Table 2-7 reports the number of federal jobs at GS-14 in the sampled occupations. For the broad occupation group of "professional" the jobs surveyed by the BLS constitute nearly half of all the professional positions at GS-14 in federal employment. It seems reasonable then that in the comparability exercises, the weighted average of the survey salaries (federal employment weights are used) would fairly represent private sector professional pay for the whole class of professionals.[39]

It is quite another story for administrative personnel at GS-14. There are 30,204 GS-14 jobs classified in the broad occupation "administrative," of which only 322 are personnel directors, which is the only private sector job whose salary is used in the BLS survey. Even if the average salary for personnel director computed in the survey is right on the mark, one must still question how representative that average is of the other 99 percent of federal administrators in GS-14.

This problem is compounded when the overall GS-14 salary is computed under the comparability procedure. The salary averages for the major occupational groups (administrative and professional at GS-

39. The average would be distorted only if the occupations of attorney, chemist, accountant, and engineer were somehow unrepresentative of the average professional worker or if the sampled industries were unrepresentative of the private sector. For example, some critics have objected to BLS excluding small firms from the scope of the survey. And one might raise an eyebrow at the survey's exclusion of law firms when assessing attorneys' salaries. For most white-collar occupations, however, it would be impossible to find jobs in small firms comparable to jobs in the federal government.

14) are weighted by employment in each group to arrive at an overall average for GS-14. This means that the sample data on personnel directors—based on 115 disperse observations—are given a weight of approximately *one-half* (see middle column in table 2-7) in calculating the overall private sector average GS-14 wage. One questions whether such a small sampling ought to be relied on so heavily in determining the salary of over 50,000 federal workers in this grade. This is no trivial matter. If, in 1980, only the actually sampled jobs were used as weights (instead of making the personnel directors' salary average represent that of one-half of the GS-14s who were in administrative jobs), the GS-14 average for the private sector would have been $45,220 rather than $47,495 (a difference of 5 percent), as computed in the comparability process.

Note that I am not contending here that there is any particular direction to a possible misestimate of GS-14 pay, but rather that too heavy reliance is being placed on possibly unrepresentative data. Since for the period 1975–80 the annual salary increases of personnel directors exceeded those of any of the other eleven PAT major occupations surveyed by the BLS, it is important that other jobs be sampled to make sure that such uncommonly high average increases are in fact representative of managerial wages in the private sector.

The problem of how representative the sampled occupations are occurs throughout the BLS survey. In some instances it would not be possible to sample a reasonable number of occupations and still cover a sizable proportion of the federal work force. In other instances, there are not enough private sector jobs that are comparable to provide valid statistics. All these factors strengthen the case for including state and local government workers in the BLS survey, a proposal discussed in chapter 4.

Conclusion

This chapter has raised several issues that any pay reform proposal ought to address. There is, first of all, ample evidence that restraint on general schedule pay increases in the 1970s has opened a sizable gap between federal and private salaries at the higher GS grades. At the same time, the uniformity of GS pay rates across occupations has allowed some clerical workers in middle-level grades to be overpaid, whereas entry-level professionals and administrators are underpaid. Too-low pay rates for entry-level professionals give rise to rapid promotions and, when combined with personnel limits, lead to upward grade creep in the federal pay structure. Ultimately the distortions in pay structure can lead to the worst of all possible worlds: a low-quality work force, all bunched at high grades and thus costing too much. This outcome, fortunately, does not happen all at once, and it does not describe the current state of the federal work force. But the process of deterioration in the quality of the work force has probably begun, and it will accelerate unless pay and employment policies are changed.

Chapter Three

Pensions

THE MOST important nonsalary benefit available to federal employees is civil service retirement. This pension system, established in 1920 and available to all general schedule employees as well as to blue-collar, legislative, and Postal Service employees, replaces both social security and supplementary private pensions that typify private sector employment.

By 1980 more than 1.2 million people were on the retirement (and disability) rolls of the system (table 3-1)—an 88 percent increase over the 1970 number of beneficiaries. During the same decade annual disbursements to retirees and survivors rose from $2.52 billion to $14.55 billion, a 477 percent increase. In recent years the average new retiree under the CSR system has been in the late fifties and has worked over twenty-five years for the government. The average annual initial benefit of retirees rose 178 percent in the decade ending in 1980.

The CSR program is a big item in the federal budget. At nearly $15 billion in 1980, outlays for federal retirees were more than double federal outlays for welfare (aid to families with dependent children). CSR has grown much faster than total federal outlays—rising from 1.3 percent of the budget in 1970 to 2.5 percent in 1980. And yet relatively little public discussion of this important program has taken place.

Cost and Value

The apparent lack of concern over civil service retirement stems in large part from its unique financing, which gives the illusion of a system in "good shape," especially when contrasted to the "troubled" social security system. This illusion has prevented a sensible assessment of the true costs of the retirement program to the government.

TABLE 3-1. *Number of Annuitants on Roll and New Annuitants by Age, Service, and Benefit Payments, Civil Service Retirement and Disability Systems, Selected Fiscal Years, 1960–80*

| Fiscal year | Annuitants | New annuitants | | | | Payments to retired employees and survivors (billions of dollars) |
		Number	Average age	Average service	Average initial annuity (dollars)	
1960	396,523	50,228	61.6	21.0	2,244	1.00[a]
1970	662,223	65,313	59.7	24.4	4,236	2.52
1975	989,786	99,767	57.7	25.1	7,164	6.96
1980	1,247,886	101,959	58.6	27.4	11,772	14.55

Source: Office of Personnel Management, Compensation Group, "Federal Fringe Benefit Facts, 1980" (OPM, 1981).
a. Estimated.

The Cost to the Taxpayer

Table 3-2 reports the salient operating flows of funds into and out of the Civil Service Retirement and Disability Fund, a trust fund operated by the Office of Personnel Management that is the collector and disburser of retirement funds. The sources of income to the fund are the amount withheld from employees (currently 7 percent of pay), an equal amount contributed by the employing agency, an appropriation based on liquidating (and paying interest on) increases in the system's liability resulting from benefit increases since 1969, and interest received from trust fund holdings of Treasury securities. This combination of receipts exceeded outlays, which are primarily for benefit payments, every year in the 1970–80 decade and allowed the cumulative trust fund balance to mount to $74 billion by the end of 1980, thus covering annual outlays by about five times. (Social security's [OASI] fund balance at the end of 1980 covered only 24 percent of its annual outlays.) Moreover, these surpluses are projected to continue, allowing the cumulative balance in the CSR fund to cover outlays quite comfortably for years to come.

This comforting story totally misrepresents the costs of CSR to the government and the taxpayer. In 1980 about 80 percent of the receipts of the CSR fund were simply internal transactions of the government. While they raised the income (and the surplus) of the CSR fund, they raised outlays (and the deficit) on other government accounts. For

TABLE 3-2. *Operating Receipts and Disbursements, Civil Service Retirement and Disability Fund, Fiscal Years 1970, 1980, 1986*
Billions of dollars

Item	1970	1980	1986[a]
Receipts			
Employee contributions	1.740	3.686	5.6
Government appropriations, employer payment, and other	1.953	15.562	26.7
Interest received	0.990	5.141	10.6
Total	4.683	24.389	42.9
Disbursements			
Benefit payments			
Retirees	2.129	12.638	n.a.
Survivors	0.389	1.912	n.a.
Refunds and death claims	0.226	0.396	n.a.
Administrative expense	0.007	0.030	n.a.
Transfers to other retirement systems	. . .	0.001	n.a.
Total	2.752	14.978	30.1
Surplus	1.931	9.411	12.8
Balance in fund, end of year	22.400	73.700	134.0[b]

Sources: For 1970 and 1980, OPM, Compensation Group, "Fringe Benefits"; for 1986, Congressional Budget Office, *Civil Service Retirement: Financing and Costs* (Government Printing Office, 1981), pp. 23, 43.
n.a. Not available.
a. Projected figures.
b. Author's estimate, based on second source above.

example, the $5 billion receipt of interest by the CSR fund in 1980 was matched by an outlay of $5 billion in interest payments by the Treasury. The net effect of this transfer on budget outlays is nil.

The budget effect of the CSR system becomes much clearer when all the intragovernmental transfers are eliminated (table 3-3). The only unambiguous receipts (from outside the government) of the system are the contributions by federal employees of 7 percent of pay. In addition, since the U.S. Postal Service is now classified as an off-budget agency, its payments to the CSR fund are "receipts from outside" insofar as the unified budget is concerned.[1] The net effect of CSR on the federal budget is far from comforting: the annual deficit attributable to CSR rose from

1. The combined deficit of the unified budget and the off-budget entities determine the government's need to borrow from the public. Thus an increase in Postal Service payments to CSR would reduce the unified budget deficit, but if the increased payment was offset by a larger subsidy to the Postal Service, borrowing from the public would be unaffected. See Congressional Budget Office, *Civil Service Retirement: Financing and Costs* (Government Printing Office, 1981), chap. 2.

TABLE 3-3. *Effect of the Civil Service Retirement System on the Unified Budget, Fiscal Years 1970, 1980, 1986*
Billions of dollars

Item	1970	1980	1986[a]
Receipts			
Employee contributions	1.740	3.686	5.6
Payments from off-budget agencies	. . .	1.489	2.3
Total	1.740	5.175	7.9
Payments to the public	2.752	14.978	30.1
Deficit effect	1.012	9.803	22.2

Sources: Same as table 3-2.
a. Projected figures.

$1 billion in 1970 to nearly $10 billion in 1980 and is projected to more than double to $22 billion in 1986. These are the amounts that taxpayers must contribute (concurrently or in the future) to fulfill the government's retirement commitments to employees. This burden, although only about 1.5 percent of total federal spending in 1980, is significant, especially in contrast to the surplus that arises when the CSR fund is viewed inclusive of intragovernmental transfers.[2]

Unfortunately, even the net effect on the budget does not really convey the costs being incurred in any year by the government on behalf of its employees. Benefit payments in any year are the result of *past* employment, salary, and benefit rule decisions. Contributions exacted from today's employees, which partially offset benefit payment costs, reflect only this year's employment level, contribution rate, and average salary. What is needed to measure a given year's cost of CSR is an estimate of the benefits ever to be paid to that year's employee cohort and an estimate of those employees' total contributions.

The actuarial concept of normal cost comes closest to representing the cost to the government (taxpayer) of the CSR. Normal cost valuations, as under the methodology of the Board of Actuaries of the Civil Service Retirement System, are done by applying to the current cohort of covered active employees (distributed by age, sex, and salary) assumptions based on recent experience about (a) rates of withdrawal

2. For a complete history of the fund as well as a readable discussion of its actuarial position, see Staff of the Bureau of Retirement, Insurance, and Occupational Health of the Civil Service Commission, "Study of Financing of the Civil Service Retirement System," in Dan M. McGill, ed., *Financing the Civil Service Retirement System: A Threat to Fiscal Integrity* (Richard D. Irwin, 1979).

TABLE 3-4. *Normal Cost of Civil Service Retirement as Percent of Payroll, Fiscal Year 1977*

Item	Percent of payroll
Annuities to employees	29.4
Optional retirement	20.7
Disability	5.1
Involuntary retirement	3.2
Deferred separation	0.4
Annuities to survivors	5.6
Lump-sum payments	1.0
Additional benefits for certain groups	0.5
Administrative expenses	0.1
Gross normal costs	36.5
Current employee contribution rate	7.0
Employer share normal cost	29.5

Source: *Board of Actuaries of the Civil Service Retirement System Fifty-Seventh Annual Report,* Committee Print, House Committee on Post Office and Civil Service, 96 Cong. 2 sess. (GPO, 1980), p. 14.

from employment, retirement and disability, mortality rates, and rates of salary increase excluding inflation (that is, promotion and step increases only) and (b) economic assumptions, based on historical data and judgment, about inflation, salary schedule increases, and interest rates. When combined with current age-service rules determining benefits, these assumptions yield estimates of a stream of expected benefit payments in the future. The stream of benefits is then discounted by the assumed interest rate (giving a present value) as is the projected payroll of active employees. The ratio of the present value of the benefits to the present value of payroll is the (gross) normal cost of the retirement system. It shows what fraction of payroll would have to be set aside in a fund each year so that the fund would be just sufficient to meet all anticipated benefit payments.

Normal cost estimates made by the Board of Actuaries based on federal work-force characteristics in fiscal 1977 are shown in table 3-4. The central economic assumptions used for this valuation are annual inflation (consumer price index) increases of 6.0 percent, annual salary schedule increases of 6.5 percent, and annual interest rates of 7.0 percent.[3] Under these assumptions the percent of payroll that would have to be set aside to fund the current age-service based, indexed civil

3. In addition, employees' salaries were assumed to increase annually by 2.3 percent for promotion and step increases between ages thirty and sixty.

service retirement system is 36.5 percent.[4] Since employees under current law contribute 7 percent of salary each year, the employer share of normal cost can be estimated at 29.5 percent of payroll. To say the same thing another way: employees pay about one-fifth of the cost of their CSR benefits; the rest comes from the taxpayer in one form or another.

The Value to Federal Employees

The normal cost estimates are based on *system* costs. They give the average percent of payroll needed to fund the CSR system. But this does not mean that each federal employee covered by CSR shares benefits in direct proportion to salary. Although the annuity is based in part on high-3 average salary (see chapter 1), it is also based on length of service, which exhibits large systematic differences for different employee groups. Moreover, some employees never become eligible for an annuity. For example, at one extreme is the worker who enters the federal service and quits in less than five years. That person is eligible to be refunded his contribution plus 3 percent interest. Obviously, CSR is making a "profit" on such employees, and that profit holds down the percent of payroll needed to fund those who do qualify for annuities.

An example of the varied outcomes under CSR can be seen by examining data on "optional retirees" entering the CSR retirement rolls in 1980. These are people who voluntarily retire directly from federal employment, and they account for two-thirds of all new retirees. Table 3-5 reports the characteristics of such retirees by the provision under which they retired. The first category represents people who have spent almost all their working lives (thirty-five years on average) with the

4. Some people find this number unbelievably high and think the actuaries are pulling a fast one. But this result can be reached intuitively as well. Forget about interest, inflation, and wage growth. Suppose wages are w and a career spans thirty years. Then $30w$ is lifetime wages. Life expectancy at retirement for a federal employee (the average new retiree is in his late fifties) is about twenty years. After working thirty years in the government, the employee is entitled to an annuity of about half of salary (see chapter 1). So, if k is the annual percent of salary needed to fund retirement, then

$$\frac{k30w}{20} = \frac{w}{2}.$$

(The fund built up at retirement divided by twenty years of life expectancy equals half of salary.) Solving the equation gives $k = 0.33$. This is close to the actuaries' calculation of 36.5 percent.

TABLE 3-5. *Characteristics of Optional Retirees Entering the Civil Service Retirement Rolls in Fiscal Year 1980*

Retirement group	Men	Women	Average years of service	Average age at issue	Average initial annuity (dollars)	Implied final salary (dollars)	CSR wealth (dollars)	Ratio of CSR wealth to final salary	Replacement rate	Percent of employee pay required to fund CSR wealth
30 years service, age 55 or over	39,288	6,108	34.8	59.1	15,429	25,492	282,196	11.1	60.5	41.6
20–29 years service, age 60 or over	3,886	2,020	25.3	60.7	9,720	22,573	167,437	7.4	43.1	35.6
12–29 years service, age 62 or over	9,896	4,918	20.6	64.8	7,416	21,545	111,033	5.2	34.4	29.3
5 years service, age 62 or over	1,176	928	9.4	64.8	2,796	20,013	41,862	2.1	14.0	23.8

Sources: OPM, Compensation Group, "Fringe Benefits"; and author's calculations (see appendix B).

government. They are able to retire at a relatively young age (fifty-nine on average), and are predominantly (about 87 percent) males whose final salary is equivalent to GS-11. The next category, people who retire under the eligibility provision for retirement at age sixty with twenty years of service, tend to retire at a slightly later age (about sixty-one years), have less service (twenty-five years), are less predominantly male, and have attained a final salary equivalent to GS-10. Finally, under the eligibility rule that allows people to retire at age sixty-two with five years of service is found a much higher representation of women, who retire relatively late (about age sixty-five), have relatively short government careers (under twenty years on average), and have attained a salary equivalent to GS-8 or GS-9 (bottom two rows of table 3-5). These groups can be characterized as male professional-administrative careerists; female and male, interrupted service, professional-administrative careerists; and female and male clerical-technical part-careerists.

For each of these groups, I have estimated the implications of the civil service retirement system, using the same assumptions as the Board of Actuaries. The assumptions and derivation of these results are explained in appendix B.

For full-career employees the CSR system is generous indeed. Such employees reach retirement with an implicit fund set aside to finance their annuity (CSR wealth), whose value is about eleven times final salary (table 3-5). Over 60 percent of their final salary is replaced by their annuity. If a constant fraction of this group's own salary had been set aside to provide retirement benefits, the fraction would have had to be 41.6 percent.[5]

For interrupted careerists the system also provides substantial benefits. CSR wealth is about 7.4 times final salary, and the CSR annuity replaces about 43 percent of final preretirement pay. To accumulate a fund adequate to support these payments would have required a level 36 percent of these employees' salaries to be set aside.

The clerical-technical partial career group is served much less well by civil service retirement. They retire relatively later in life after a relatively short career—resulting in CSR wealth accumulation of two to

5. These calculations all assume that the Board of Actuaries' assumptions about the future also apply to the past. But the crucial assumptions are the real rate of interest and real wage growth (as shown in appendix B). These assumptions of the board (1 percent real interest, 2.8 percent real wage growth) are not out of line with past experience.

five times final salary. Annuities replace about one-third of preretirement pay for those who put in about twenty years, but only one-seventh of pay for those with ten years of service. If these employees' pay had been debited each year to reflect the needed accumulation of wealth by retirement, about 25 percent of pay would have been deducted.

This review gives some of the flavor of the divergences in payoff to different groups of federal employees.[6] Even within the same assumptions that lead to an employer (gross) normal cost of 36.5 percent of payroll, some career employees may be benefiting closer to 43 percent of pay and some clerical-technical employees with shorter federal careers may be getting only about 25 percent of pay in the form of deferred compensation. There is of course nothing wrong with retirement programs that confer greatest benefits on career employees; indeed, retirement plans should probably be designed on the assumption that employees will work full careers. But the disparities in the benefits of the CSR have implications for a number of reform programs that are reviewed in the next chapter.

Is Civil Service Retirement Too Costly?

It is one thing to associate a cost figure with CSR, but another to evaluate whether that cost is high or low. In the following sections I use three standards of evaluation. First, costs to the employer for CSR are compared with costs for private sector retirement plans. Second, CSR is evaluated for its adequacy in replacing preretirement income. Third, the value of federal and private sector retirement to various groups of employees is compared.

Employer Cost

As already noted, the gross normal cost of the CSR system when evaluated by the Board of Actuaries of the Civil Service Retirement Fund in 1977 was 36.5 percent of payroll. Since employees contribute 7 percent of salary to the fund each year, the normal cost to the employer can be estimated at 29.5 percent of payroll. This bottom-line figure

6. Even more extreme divergences can be demonstrated when deferred annuities are considered, as seen later in the chapter.

implicitly assumes that federal employees' salaries are unaffected by the retirement system's characteristics and that the ultimate incidence of costs to these employees is limited to the current 7 percent contribution (which in turn is implicitly assumed never to change). This is consistent with the process by which federal salaries are set: pensions play no explicit role.

Private sector pension costs present enormous problems to the evaluator. The following analysis relies on the methodology and data used by the Office of Personnel Management (OPM),[7] but some alternatives are considered. Virtually all private sector workers are covered by social security, and many are also employed by firms with pension plans.

To evaluate the costs to the employer of social security, the OPM first computes a gross normal cost for social security (old age, survivors, and disability only—not medicare) based on the same economic assumptions and same characteristics of work-force retirement, promotion, and so on, that were used by the Board of Actuaries to evaluate civil service retirement. The resulting gross normal cost for social security is 16.4 percent of payroll and can be interpreted as the total cost of providing social security to a work force with the characteristics of the federal work force. To establish the employer's share of this gross normal cost, OPM assumes from "current legislation and past experience" that half the gross cost is borne by employees and half by the employer. Thus the employer cost of social security is estimated at 8.2 percent of payroll.[8] This estimate implicitly assumes that current employer and employee costs of 4.7 percent of payroll[9] will each rise to 8.2 percent and that these increases will have no effect on salary growth or prices in the private sector. Most economic analysis would not point toward that result. For if payroll taxes rise, some combination of a diminution in wage growth and acceleration in price level will probably occur, leaving real private sector compensation (wage plus payroll tax) unchanged.[10] Such a reduc-

7. See Office of Personnel and Management, Compensation Group, "Total Compensation Comparability: Background, Method, Preliminary Results" (July 1981).

8. Ibid., pp. 14, 18.

9. This fraction is below the 6.5 percent total payroll tax rate in 1980 because (a) 1.05 percentage points of that tax are currently channeled to medicare, and (b) the payroll tax is applied only to earnings below the wage base ($25,900 in 1980). See Social Security Bulletin, vol. 43 (September 1980), p. 11.

10. See John A. Brittain, The Payroll Tax for Social Security (Brookings Institution, 1972), especially chap. 2.

tion in the growth of real wages will raise the normal cost of social security.[11]

Alternatively, as a report prepared by the Congressional Budget Office suggested, since the OPM uses the current statutory rate of 7 percent to estimate employee cost in the CSR system, the statutory rates (including future statutory increases) ought to be used for employee cost in social security. According to the budget office, this statutory rate works out to 5 percent of payroll, which would raise employer cost to over 11 percent. (The Social Security Administration estimates are 6 percent for employees and 10 percent for employers.)[12]

Private pension plan data of a comprehensive kind first became available to the OPM in 1980. In that year the Bureau of Labor Statistics salary survey used for the pay comparability calculations was broadened to include some nonsalary benefits, including pensions. Private pension plan benefit rules (age of retirement, amount of pension, rule for vesting, and so forth) were applied to the federal work force to ascertain the gross normal cost of private pensions, once again by using the same economic assumptions as were used to estimate the normal cost of CSR. According to the OPM, the gross normal cost of private pensions was 6.4 percent of payroll.[13] Since there are rarely any employee contributions to private pension plans, no deductions are made for employee contributions, so that net employer cost is estimated to be 6.4 percent of payroll.

All the questions about who actually pays for pensions that were raised for social security can be raised here—for example, have private sector wages been held down because of pension benefits? Furthermore, the numerous conflicting reports of underfunding of private pension plans bring up another issue.[14] If such plans are inadequately funded currently and if corporations are forced to increase their contributions

11. Costs of social security increase in response to declining real wage growth, because the smaller wage base diminishes the earnings of the system during the worker's accumulation period and because more rapid price increases would raise the indexed retirement benefits. *1981 Annual Report of the Board of Trustees of the Federal Old-Age and Survivors Insurance and Disability Insurance Trust Funds*, p. 90.

12. See Congressional Budget Office, *Compensation Reform for Federal White-Collar Employees: The Administration's Proposal and Budgetary Options for 1981* (GPO, 1980), p. 24; and *Social Security Bulletin*, vol. 43 (September 1980), p. 11.

13. OPM, Compensation Group, "Total Compensation Comparability," p. 18.

14. For a discussion of various accounting procedures that lead to differing conclusions about pension underfunding, see Alicia H. Munnell, *The Economics of Private Pensions* (Brookings Institution, 1982), chap. 6.

TABLE 3-6. *Participation in Private Pension Plans by Size of Establishment, Private Nonfarm Wage and Salary Workers, 1979*

Workers	Number (millions)	Percent distribution
Participants	31.6	45.7
Nonparticipants	37.6	54.3
Less than 25 employees	21.1	30.4
25–99 employees	8.3	12.0
100 or more employees	8.2	11.8
Total	69.2	100.0

Source: May 1979 Current Population Survey data from ICF, Inc., "Background Analysis of the Potential Effects of a Minimum Universal Pension System (MUPS)" (April 15, 1981), pp. 6, 14.

in the future, this might affect future wage growth and the estimated normal cost of the plans.

An additional caveat is also in order concerning the scope of the BLS survey with regard to pension cost estimates. About 54 percent of the employees in the private nonfarm economy do not participate in a private pension program (table 3-6). These workers are highly concentrated in small firms: nearly a third of the private work force is in establishments with fewer than 25 employees that have no private pension program at all. The BLS survey of private firms does not sample companies with fewer than 50, 100, or 250 employees, depending on industry. This means that, at a minimum, the nearly one-third of all workers whose pension plans are known to have a normal cost of zero are systematically excluded from the survey. It follows that the OPM estimate of 6.4 percent of payroll probably overstates the employer normal cost for the private nonfarm wage and salary work force. On the other hand, state and local government pension plans, many of which rival the CSR plan in generosity,[15] are not included in the survey either.

The result of the OPM's estimate of employer's costs for retirement programs in the federal and private sector is shown in table 3-7. The employer cost of the federal retirement program is estimated at about 14 percent of payroll above that of the private sector. Even with the questions raised in this section about the data and about the conceptual problems of allocating costs between employer and employee, it is hard to escape the conclusion that the CSR plan costs the government much

15. See *Pension Task Force Report on Public Employees Retirement Systems,* Committee Print, House Committee on Education and Labor, 95 Cong. 2 sess. (GPO, 1978), p. 122.

TABLE 3-7. *Comparison of Employer Cost of Retirement Benefits in Federal and Private Sectors, 1980*
Percent of payroll

Cost	Federal	Private	Percent difference
Gross normal cost			
Civil service retirement	35.2	. . .	. . .
Social security	. . .	16.4	. . .
Private pensions	. . .	6.5[a]	. . .
Total	35.2	22.9	12.3
Employee contribution			
Civil service retirement	7.0	. . .	. . .
Social security	. . .	8.2	. . .
Private pensions	. . .	. . .	. . .
Total	7.0	8.2	− 1.2
Employer cost	28.2	14.7	13.5

Source: Office of Personnel Management, Compensation Group, "Total Compensation Comparability: Background, Method, Preliminary Results" (July 1981).
a. Includes 0.1 for long-term disability.

more than social security and private pensions cost employers. This does not necessarily imply that federal retirement is "too costly"—it may be that private pensions are too skimpy. But CSR is clearly out of line with retirement costs in the private sector.

Adequacy of Retirement Benefits

An alternative way to measure the degree of adequacy of CSR is to assess its ability to meet retirement income goals. These goals are usually expressed in terms of the replacement rate, the ratio of the initial pension to the last year of preretirement income. To establish an adequate replacement ratio requires two steps: first, determining the consumption (that is, spendable income, not needed for savings) rate out of preretirement income, and second, determining the fraction of the consumption rate that should be replaced. Fortunately, the President's Commission on Pension Policy has recently analyzed these questions, and its studies can provide a basis for evaluating retirement plans.

According to the commission, a single person in the salary range $10,000 to $50,000 who enters retirement would require replacement rates between 44 and 73 percent of final salary (table 3-8).[16] The higher

16. Income levels below $10,000 (where the required replacement rate is higher) are omitted because virtually no federal career employee would reach retirement at a salary below this amount.

TABLE 3-8. *Level of Consumption Needed in Retirement to Maintain Preretirement Consumption Level, 1980*

Dollars unless otherwise specified

1980 salary	Preretirement taxes and savings			Consumption level needed in retirement	
	Income and payroll tax[a]	Work-related expenses	Savings	Amount	Replacement rate on 1980 salary (percent)
Single person					
10,000	2,008	480	240	7,272	72.7
15,000	3,703	678	678	9,941	66.3
20,000	5,783	853	1,280	12,084	60.4
30,000	10,355[b]	1,179	2,357[b]	16,109	53.7
50,000	22,249[b]	1,665	4,163[b]	21,923	43.8
Married couple, one earner					
10,000	1,444	513	257	7,786	77.9
15,000	2,860	728	728	10,684	71.2
20,000	4,488	931	1,396	13,185	65.9
30,000	8,047[b]	1,317	2,634[b]	18,002[c]	60.0
50,000	17,824[b]	1,931	4,826[b]	25,419	50.8

Source: President's Commission on Pension Policy, *Coming of Age: Toward a National Retirement Income Policy* (GPO, 1981), pp. 42–43.

a. Payroll tax is social security.

b. For federal worker, computation assumes that excess of CSR contribution over social security contribution at high incomes is reflected in savings column.

c. Corrected from source.

percentage applies at the $10,000 salary primarily because such employees are assumed to be relatively lightly taxed before retirement; thus they probably spent a large share of their preretirement salary on consumer goods and services. At the $50,000 income, by contrast, the preretirement tax bite (for single persons especially) is sharply higher, and the commission assumes that preretirement savings rates are higher as well.[17] The result of these assumptions is that a high-salaried single person may be spending as little as 44 percent of salary on consumer goods and services just before retirement.

A similar set of estimates for married couples, with one earner, shows rates of preretirement consumption spending ranging from 51 percent to 78 percent of salary. Married couples have these higher rates because it

17. The commission assumes savings rates out of after-tax income of 3, 6, 9, 12, and 15 percent, respectively, for the five salary levels shown in table 3-8. President's Commission on Pension Policy, *Coming of Age: Toward a National Retirement Income Policy* (GPO, 1981), p. 29.

TABLE 3-9. *Adequacy of Replacement Rates under Civil Service Retirement and Social Security for Single Persons, 1980*
Percent

1980 salary	Full consumption replacement rate[a] (1)	CSR after-tax replacement rate (2)	Social security replacement rate (3)	Index of adequacy of CSR[b] (4)	Index of adequacy of social security[c] (5)	Replacement rate needed to raise social security benefit to CSR standard	
						After tax (6)	Before tax (7)
10,000	73	61	49	85	67	12	12
15,000	66	59	42	89	63	17	17
20,000	60	58	34	96	56	24	24
30,000	54	56	23	104	43	33	36
50,000	44	53	14	120	32	39	46

Sources: For column 1, President's Commission on Pension Policy, *Coming of Age*, pp. 42–43; for column 2, author's estimate as explained in note a; for column 3, President's Commission on Pension Policy, "An Interim Report" (November 1980), p. 29.

a. Based on thirty-five years of service; assumes high-3 average salary is 94 percent of 1980 salary. Federal tax computed from 1980 tax form assumes that 80 percent of CSR annuity is taxable, that retiree is sixty-five years or older, that deductions equal average itemized deductions for gross income class, and that no payroll tax is payable. Average deductions are from Academic Information Service, *1981 Tax Guide for College Teachers* (AIS, 1980), p. 154.

b. CSR after-tax replacement rate (column 2) divided by full consumption replacement rate (col. 1) times 100.

c. Social security replacement rate (column 3) divided by full consumption replacement rate (col. 1) times 100.

is presumed that at any given earnings level they pay lower taxes than single workers do.

Replacement rates needed to maintain consumption at preretirement levels are frequently used to assess the adequacy of a retirement program, ordinarily thought to consist of social security, employer pensions, and private savings for private sector workers. The President's Commission on Pension Policy stated that "a desirable retirement income goal" would be to replace enough preretirement income so that people were "able to maintain their preretirement living standard during retirement years."[18] This means that the combination of all retirement income sources would have to produce enough disposable (after-tax) income to generate a replacement rate in retirement equal to the rate shown in the first columns of tables 3-9 and 3-10 (which correspond to the last column of table 3-8).

How does civil service retirement measure up to this ambitious

18. Ibid., pp. 41–42.

TABLE 3-10. *Adequacy of Replacement Rates under Civil Service Retirement and Social Security for Married Persons, 1980*
Percent

1980 salary	Full consumption replacement rate (1)	CSR after-tax replacement rate[a] (2)	Social security replacement rate (3)	Index of adequacy of CSR[b] (4)	Index of adequacy of social security[c] (5)	Replacement rate needed to raise social security benefit to CSR standard	
						After tax (6)	Before tax (7)
10,000	78	62	73	80	94	0	0
15,000	71	62	64	88	89	0	0
20,000	66	61	51	92	77	10	10
30,000	60	58	34	97	57	24	24
50,000	51	56	21	110	41	35	39

Sources: Same as table 3-9.
a. See table 3-9, note a.
b. See table 3-9, note b.
c. See table 3-9, note c.

standard?[19] For a worker employed by the federal government for thirty-five years with a final salary in excess of $30,000, the CSR retirement pension (after a deduction for federal taxes due) will fully replace the preretirement consumption standard (tables 3-9 and 3-10). In fact, at the highest salary level ($50,000) a single federal worker may receive an after-tax retirement income that will support as much as 20 percent more consumption than in the year before retirement. The corresponding excess would be about 10 percent for a married worker with a $50,000 final salary (tables 3-9 and 3-10). (The difference occurs because the single worker's preretirement tax rate, unlike that of a person filing a joint return, is much higher than his postretirement tax rate.)

At the bottom end of the federal workers' pay scale, CSR annuities alone are not enough to support preretirement consumption, even for a worker who has put in thirty-five years of federal service. At the $10,000

19. Replacement of all preretirement consumption is ambitious; it assumes that throughout retirement a person would consume as much as in his last working year, which is likely to have been the highest consumption level of the previous, say, thirty-five years. Thus, for example, if real consumption rises 2 percent a year during a work life spanning ages twenty through sixty, full replacement of consumption at age sixty means that real retirement consumption levels would exceed the *average* (not final year) real consumption during the work career by about 40 to 50 percent.

to $15,000 final salary level, a federal retiree could expect that his after-tax CSR benefit would support between 80 and 90 percent of preretirement consumption.

Thus, when measured against estimated preretirement consumption standards, the civil service retirement system alone provides benefits to full-career workers that are more than adequate for the highest-grade ($30,000–$50,000 salary) employees and somewhat less than adequate for employees retiring at salaries at or below $15,000 in 1980. Single workers generally are better able to maintain consumption standards than married ones. These estimates presume that civil service retirement is the only source of retirement income to federal annuitants. However, all available evidence indicates that a great many civil service retirees also qualify for social security. This is true even of those civil servants who worked for thirty or more years for the federal government. In 1975, for example, 98,000 civil service annuitants who each had over thirty years of civil service employment also qualified for social security benefits. About 70 percent of these annuitants qualified for relatively small social security benefits (because they were covered by social security employment for ten years or less),[20] which nevertheless added to the possibilities of their retirement period consumption. But for those annuitants who had worked ten years in covered employment, the payoff in extra social security benefits could be enormous (table 3-11). For example, low-income federal career ($10,000 salary) workers who qualified for social security in 1975 will get back three to four times the social security taxes they contributed, which will significantly reduce the inadequacy of the CSR annuity taken alone. And even high-income employees ($30,000–$50,000) will get back double the social security taxes they paid; for such workers, the opportunity to qualify under social security can be viewed as a high-payoff savings plan not available to other high-income workers. The possibility of federal workers adding to their civil service retirement income through coverage under social security appears to be growing. According to the Social Security Administration, over 70 percent of the 1979 CSR annuitants were currently (or would subsequently be) eligible for social security benefits. And one

20. All data are from Department of Health, Education, and Welfare, Universal Social Security Coverage Study Group, "Report: The Desirability and Feasibility of Social Security Coverage for Employees of Federal, State and Local Governments and Private Non Profit Organizations" (March 1980), pp. 37–41.

TABLE 3-11. *Ratio of Employee Primary Benefits Accrued to Social Security Taxes Paid for Workers with Ten and Twenty Years of Covered Earnings, Selected Final Salary Levels, 1975*

Years of career covered by social security	Final salary (dollars)				
	10,000	15,000	20,000	30,000	50,000
Last ten	3.9	3.3	2.8	2.4	2.1
First ten	3.2	2.8	2.5	2.1	1.8
Last twenty	2.7	2.2	2.0	1.8	1.5
First twenty	2.3	2.0	1.8	1.6	1.4

Source: Department of Health, Education, and Welfare, Universal Social Security Coverage Study Group, "Report: The Desirability and Feasibility of Social Security Coverage for Employees of Federal, State and Local Governments and Private Non Profit Organizations" (March 1980), pp. 37–41.

study showed that 80 percent of younger CSR annuitants were potential social security beneficiaries.[21]

In sum, it is hard not to conclude that present CSR benefits are more than adequate to meet maintenance of consumption standards for higher-salaried federal workers retiring after a full career. For full-career workers who retire at low salaries, the CSR benefits alone fall somewhat short of maintaining preretirement consumption standards, but if they are supplemented by social security benefits, any drop in living standards would probably be negligible. Finally, even for federal employees who retire with less than full careers, the chances of retirement earnings meeting preretirement standards are not bad if the possibility of qualifying for social security is considered. Roughly speaking, for each ten years not spent in a federal job, the (after-tax) replacement rates provided by the CSR annuity would fall by 17 to 20 percentage points (if the ten years were early in the career). Thus CSR alone would be an inadequate replacement for a twenty-five-year career even at high salary levels. But if the lost time in federal employment was spent in covered social security, the worker could recapture most (and at lower incomes, all) of the lost CSR benefit in enhanced social security benefits.[22] Thus, except in unusual cases—people who do not work at all for a large part of their

21. Ibid., p. 41. Data refer to all CSR annuitants, not just those with long federal careers.

22. For example, a single worker with a $15,000 final salary who spent ten years in covered employment would receive social security benefits of about half what he would have received had he worked forty years under social security. This would replace about 20 percent of final salary. See ibid., pp. 33, 36.

preretirement career and those who qualify only for deferred CSR annuities—the CSR system (supplemented by social security in some cases) provides a high standard of replacement income to the federal employee. With even modest retirement income from personal savings, retired civil servants can enjoy a rising standard of living during retirement.

Federal Retirees Compared with Private Sector Retirees

Yet another way of looking at the adequacy of CSR is to compare the retirement benefits of the career civil servant with those of private sector workers with similar career earnings. Virtually all private sector workers are covered by social security, and that public pension system is the single most important source of income to most private sector retirees.

Social security benefits are structured according to different principles from CSR benefits. The social security system, by design, seeks to replace a larger share of preretirement income for low-income people than for high-income ones. (This is accomplished through a benefit formula that replaces more of average earnings in lower brackets than in higher ones.) Moreover, the system is designed to be of special benefit to married couples when only one spouse has earnings. (A 50 percent addition to the primary benefit is paid when an aged spouse is present.) These attributes are illustrated by social security replacement rates at various levels of final salary in tables 3-9 and 3-10 (columns 3 and 5). For single workers with a $10,000 final salary, social security replaces about 49 percent of final salary, or about two-thirds of the preretirement consumption level. For the $15,000 (approximately average) worker social security replaces a little over 40 percent of salary, or about 63 percent of estimated consumption. The replacement of preretirement consumption drops sharply above the wage base (which in 1980 was $25,900) and declines to about one-third at a $50,000 final salary. Married workers fare better, with social security replacing over 90 percent of estimated preretirement consumption for the $10,000 employee and nearly 80 percent for the worker with a $20,000 final salary. However, the replacement of consumption then drops sharply, falling to a 41 percent replacement rate at $50,000 earnings. (No adjustments for postretirement taxation are made because social security benefits are not taxed.)

The entirely different tilt of the social security system means that if one is comparing private sector and federal employee retirement benefits, it is essential to specify income and marital status before making the comparison. The last two columns of tables 3-9 and 3-10 illustrate this point. They show that the following supplements to social security are required to raise the retirement benefits of private sector workers to the level attained by full-career CSR beneficiaries.

—Zero for married workers with final salaries under $15,000. They are better off under social security than under the civil service retirement system.

—Anywhere from 12 percent to 24 percent (before tax) of final salary for single workers up to $20,000 final salary and for married workers up to $30,000 salary.

—Very large at the upper end of the salary scale. Above $30,000 for singles and at $50,000 for married workers, 36 percent to 46 percent of final salary (before tax).

It is simply not conceivable that private pension plans are replacing gaps of the magnitude found in the upper salary brackets. Recall that the average normal cost of private pension plans is about 6.5 percent of payroll. For full-career workers, each percentage point of payroll put in a pension fund would purchase about 2.2 percentage points of replacement of final salary.[23] Thus the 6.5 percent of payroll normal cost of the average private pension plan would buy about 14.3 points of real replacement for the average worker. Although many private pension plans

23. Assume that after a thirty-five-year career the life expectancy of the worker is fifteen years. To fund equal yearly payments of x dollars for fifteen years with an assumed real interest rate of 1 percent would require a fund wealth, W, equal to $13.865x$. The annuity the worker receives is by definition equal to the replacement rate R times final salary F. Thus

$$W = R \cdot F \cdot 13.865.$$

One can compute retirement wealth as a function of final salary and contribution rate k, using the formula derived in appendix B:

$$W = F \cdot k \cdot \left[1 - \left(\frac{1+r}{1+w}\right)^m \middle/ 1 - \left(\frac{1+r}{1+w}\right) \right],$$

where m is the career length, r the nominal interest rate, and w the rate of wage increases. If one assumes $m = 35$ years, $r = 0.07$, and $w = 0.08$, the ratio in this equation equals 30.0126. One can combine the two expressions to get R in terms of k:

$$R = k \cdot \frac{30.0126}{13.8650}$$
$$R = 2.164\, k.$$

are structured to replace a higher fraction of final salary at the high salary ranges than at the lower salary levels,[24] it is hard to imagine that the average replacement rate of final salary at $50,000 would be double that at $20,000 salary in a typical private plan.[25]

Some analysts have come to a different conclusion about the comparative generosity of CSR and typical private plans by observing that initial replacement rates are similar. But a comparison of initial year replacement rates for a fully indexed CSR and the combined social security (fully indexed) and private pension (not indexed) is misleading, because the private sector replacement rate declines steadily after the initial year whereas the federal pension maintains its value throughout retirement.

This difference in the scope of the indexed portion of retirement income has a strong quantitative effect on the comparison between the two sectors. For example, an average private sector worker would receive 42 percent replacement from social security. In addition, if his pension plan set aside 6.5 percent of salary each year for thirty-five years, a fund equal to 1.95 times final salary would be available at retirement under the assumptions in note 23. If such a pension fund were invested in an ordinary, nonindexed annuity based on a 7 percent interest rate and a fifteen-year expected life, the annual fixed (nonindexed) annuity would be 21 percent of final salary. The combined initial replacement rate of 63 percent is just about equal to the CSR replacement for a thirty-five-year career (setting aside tax differences) in the first year of retirement. But if a retiree wanted to provide himself with a constant real level of consumption during retirement, he could not consume all the first year benefits of his fixed-dollar private pension. In fact, in this example the retiree would have to set aside about one-third of his pension in the first year of retirement to build a fund sufficient to overcome the inflationary erosion of his fixed pension later on. In each subsequent year he would allow consumption spending to grow with inflation, continuing to save until later in retirement. Thus the private pension's real replacement rate is not 21 percent but about 14 percent of final salary. In all previous computations in this chapter a real replacement rate was used to provide a measure of the sustainable replacement of final salary. Use of unadjusted replacement rates greatly overstates the value of private pensions.

24. This is usually accomplished through "integration with social security," wherein part of the private pension is reduced for each dollar of social security benefit.

25. In fact, the IRS prohibits corporations from skewing their retirement benefits sharply in favor of high-salaried personnel.

Conclusion

The conclusion to be drawn from this section is inescapable. The CSR system is much more costly to the federal government as employer (and to the taxpayer) than the combined social security and private pension package is to employers in the private sector. The system is too costly in that it provides replacement rates for career workers in the middle and upper salary ranges that allow such workers to enjoy a higher consumption standard than before retirement. These higher-graded federal employees almost certainly prosper in retirement compared with similarly paid private sector workers. For federal career workers at the lower end of the salary scale, CSR alone is not quite adequate to meet income needs; such workers are probably not better off in retirement than their private sector counterparts, who benefit from the strongly redistributive social security system. The workers who were found in chapter 2 to be the most *underpaid,* in other words, are well treated in retirement, whereas clerical workers, who fare best in salary, derive the least comparative advantage from CSR. This theme will be returned to in the final chapter.

Problems Caused by the System

Aside from the cost of CSR and the comparability of its benefits with those of the private sector, there are many policy problems that stem from the structure of the CSR system. A few of the major problems are discussed here.

Unfair Losses and Windfall Gains

Basing CSR benefits on the highest average salary level earned during three consecutive years of federal employment causes both unduly low returns and windfalls. Consider first the case of a person who worked for the federal government for the first twenty years of a career (say, from ages twenty through thirty-nine), attaining a final three-year salary of $12,000 (GS-14 in 1959), and who then quit to work in the private sector. Suppose that over the next twenty years, the person's private sector salary just kept pace with that of a GS-14, so that it rose to about $40,000 in 1980. At that time the person was eligible for a deferred annuity from the civil service. The annuity would be based on the product of the service factor of twenty years of work (36.25 percent) and high-3 salary of $12,000, or an annuity of $4,350. Figured as a percentage of the employee's final salary of $40,000, this annuity replaces only 11 percent of pay, a paltry retirement benefit for someone who spent half a career working for the government. If the person had never quit and had worked a full career (here forty years), the annuity would have been over 70 percent of final pay. The poor retirement replacement rate for a deferred annuitant stems from the use of a nonindexed salary in the computation of the CSR benefit—a characteristic flaw of many private pension plans as well.

Suppose that in 1980 the person, instead of retiring, goes back to work for the federal government for three years at a $40,000 salary. When he or she is ready to retire in 1983, the CSR benefit jumps to an initial level of $16,900 (45.25 service factor times high-3 of $40,000). The same high-3 rule that causes paltry benefits for a deferred pension generates an enormous return to an employee who returns to federal service just before retirement. The increased annuity that the additional three years of employment makes possible would require that the government set aside each year more than 100 percent of the salary paid to the reemployed worker.[26] It seems proper to call this a windfall gain.

Early Retirement

Federal employees who become eligible for retirement under CSR face a choice that, except in unusual circumstances, makes it financially attractive to retire from the civil service as soon as possible. Continuing in government service for an additional year brings the employee that year's salary, an additional 2 percent of high-3 salary during retirement, and a larger annuity if the high-3 average is raised. Against these emoluments are pitted the advantages of retiring from federal service: any salary received that year from private sector work, the indexed annuity for that year, the additional social security benefit qualified for

26. The $4,350 annuity would have grown to $5,790 by 1983 if it was indexed at a 10 percent inflation rate. Thus the annuity stemming from reemployment is about $11,110 higher than if reemployment did not occur. The present value (in 1983) of $11,110 over a fifteen-year expected lifetime, discounted at 1 percent real interest, is over $154,000. This fund would have to be accumulated in three years, so at any reasonable interest rate it would require annual deposits of over $40,000.

TABLE 3-12. *Distribution of Male Civil Service and Private Sector Retirees, by Age at Retirement, 1976, 1980*
Percent

Age at retirement[a]	1976		1980, civil service[d]
	Civil service[b]	Private sector[c]	
Under 55	9.5	1.1	16.6
55–59	39.6	6.3	37.0
60–61	14.5	12.6	} 34.0
62–64	18.1	42.1	
65 and over	18.3	37.9	12.5

Sources: Congressional Budget Office, *Options for Federal and Civil Service Retirement: An Analysis of Costs and Benefit Provisions* (GPO, 1978), p. 10; CBO, *Civil Service Retirement*, p. 29; and Social Security Administration, Office of Research and Statistics, *Research Report No. 47*, p. 172.

a. For private sector, age at which private pension was first received by men awarded social security retirement benefits in fiscal 1976.

b. Calculated from data on men who retired under civil service during fiscal 1976, excluding those who were disabled or who received deferred pensions.

c. Data include some men who also received civil service benefits.

d. New additions to employee retirements during fiscal 1980, prepared by CBO from data supplied by the Office of Personnel Management.

from private sector work, and any private pension rights earned. It would make financial sense to continue working for the government only if (a) the employee can substantially raise his high-3 average salary, which can be done through promotion or if the civil service pay scale is rising sharply, or (b) he cannot obtain private sector employment or has little chance of qualifying for social security, or (c) he does not gain much from getting on the indexed CSR benefit roll because inflation is low. In recent years the opposite of these conditions held for most employees becoming eligible for CSR benefits. Prices were rising faster than civil service wages, and most federal workers becoming eligible for retirement had built up enough time in covered earnings under social security so that additional private sector employment would add to the social security entitlement.[27]

The incentives have had a predictable result. By 1976 nearly half of all male civil service retirements occurred under age sixty, while less than 10 percent of the private sector males retired that young (table 3-12). Only 18 percent of civil service retirees stayed in government work until age sixty-five; double that percentage stayed on the job to the

27. For a full discussion of these factors and empirical results, see Gary Burtless and Jerry A. Hausman, " 'Double Dipping': The Combined Effects of Social Security and Civil Service Pensions on Employee Retirement," Working Paper 800 (National Bureau of Economic Research, 1981).

traditional retirement age in the private sector. By 1980 new retirees under civil service were even younger. Over half the men retired before sixty, and a minuscule 12.5 percent worked for the government after sixty-five.

These retirements at a young age by federal employees create two problems for public policy. First, from the point of view of an effective federal civil service, the loss of many people whose experience simply cannot be replaced has a serious effect. This effect is most severe in managerial positions, where years of experience may be the most important attribute. Second, by encouraging retirement at an early age for federal employees, the government is giving a dissonant signal to the private sector. Federal policy for private sector retirement is currently embodied in the rules governing social security. Those rules permit a full retirement benefit only at age sixty-five and a reduced benefit at age sixty-two. Most proposed changes in these rules would push the full benefit age to sixty-eight, to reduce the burden on the working population, which will decline dramatically relative to the elderly population early in the next century.[28] It is anomalous, to say the least, for the government to be pushing the private sector toward later retirement at the same time that it maintains a scheme for its own employees that encourages earlier retirement. The government could, of course, change the CSR rules so that employees would not be eligible to retire until a later age.

Dual Beneficiaries

As noted earlier, most civil service annuitants will eventually also qualify for social security retirement benefits. Federal employees who spend relatively few years in social security–covered employment receive a social security benefit based on their average indexed earnings. The average is computed over a thirty-five-year period; thus a short-term career in the private sector results in low average indexed earnings. Since the social security formula is tilted to provide high replacement for people with low average indexed earnings, the typical federal retiree who spends a short period working in the private sector reaps the gain

28. See, for example, the proposal for gradually phasing in the retirement age of sixty-eight beginning in the year 2000 in *Report of the 1979 Advisory Council on Social Security,* Committee Print, House Committee on Ways and Means, 96 Cong. 1 sess. (GPO, 1980), pp. 161–64.

from this tilt in the social security benefit formula. Put another way, the replacement rate received from social security under present rules for these employees exceeds the replacement rate they would have received from social security if their entire career had been spent in a job covered by it.

According to the Universal Social Security Coverage Group, for 98.6 percent of the dual beneficiaries, social security benefits represent a windfall gain (measured as the excess of the replacement rate actually received over the replacement that would have been received if the whole career had been spent in covered employment) from social security. The windfall gain averages over $700 a year for each dual beneficiary, and in the mid-1970s aggregated to about a $300 million annual cost to social security.[29]

Quasi Loans

Like most private pensions, the civil service retirement fund does not formally permit workers to borrow to use their pension rights as loan collateral. However, a little known provision of CSR amounts to a quite generous loan arrangement. CSR allows an employee who is separated or is transferred to a position that is not under CSR to receive a "refund" of all previous employee contributions. If the worker is reemployed, he will receive the full CSR pension as long as his refund plus 3 percent interest compounded annually is redeposited before retirement. These provisions mean that it is possible for an employee to arrange to have himself separated, apply for a refund, and then be immediately reemployed several times during his career.[30] For each such cycle the employee gains access to his previous contributions at a cost of only 3 percent interest, well below the market rate. Compared with a private sector worker seeking loan capital to, say, finance a child's college education, some federal employees may be considerably advantaged by the CSR refund provision. These advantages were not considered in the Office of Personnel Management's estimate of the value of civil service retirement.

29. See HEW, Universal Social Security Coverage Study Group, "Report," pp. 56–60, 97–98, and 99–143 for data in this section.

30. The separation may be as short as a month for executive branch workers. In the case of legislative branch employees, who participate optionally in CSR, the separation may be only one day if they arrange to be reappointed to their jobs and do not remain in the CSR system.

Military Service

In determining the CSR benefit, full credit for years of service is given for active military service. Since no retirement deductions are taken for military service (except for social security, whose coverage was extended to the military in 1956), the portion of a civil service retiree's pension that is due to military service credit is entirely without cost to him. Two provisions of law slightly qualify this free lunch. If the retiree receives "military retired pay" (the pension paid to veterans with twenty years of military service), he does not receive credit for service under civil service retirement for the years of military service; and when social security benefits based on military service after 1956 begin to be paid to the civil service retiree, his civil service annuity is reduced by dropping the years of service credit attributable to military service. Working the other way is a provision that allows the civil service annuitant to count years of military service even if he is paid veteran's benefits that are based on the same period of service.

Partial Solutions

Each of the problems discussed in this section can be remedied by modifying CSR benefit rules. For example, the unfair losses to deferred annuitants (and windfall gain to the reentrant) would be lessened if the CSR benefit were based on career-indexed earnings rather than on the high-3 average. And eligibility for retirement in CSR could be restructured so that it became available at later ages, or retirement at young ages could be discouraged by imposition of an earnings test (reduced benefit if one is still earning more than a minimal sum).

These changes amount to reinventing the social security system for federal employees. That is, the most desirable changes in the CSR system would be ones that would make its benefit rules conform more closely to those in place under social security. It takes only a small step (and a belief that the tilt in social security benefits should be applied to federal workers too) to conclude that the simplest way to repair CSR would be to place federal workers under social security. This is discussed in the next chapter. Suffice it to say here that if federal employees were covered, the problems of dual beneficiaries and of the proper treatment of years of military service would disappear.

Chapter Four

Reform

THE PROBLEMS of federal employee pay and retirement that were discussed in the previous two chapters have not gone undiscovered. In the past few years several high-level commissions and study groups have reviewed these issues, and some proposals for legislative reform have emerged from their findings. Before presenting my own reform agenda, I discuss some of the reports and proposals from which I drew ideas.

Recent Studies

The federal retirement system has not received the same degree of scrutiny as federal pay in task force and presidential commission reports. But the issue of federal employees' coverage under social security has attracted the attention of nearly all study groups assigned the task of assessing the nation's overall retirement plans. In this section I first discuss the three most important reports on federal compensation, then three representative reports on the retirement issue.

CIVIL SERVICE COMMISSION. In 1974–75 the Civil Service Commission undertook a broad study of the compensation of federal white-collar workers, which came out in six volumes.[1] The reports in this study on the organization and salary of general schedule workers have strongly influenced all subsequent proposals. The commission found that the practice of placing all occupational groups in a single general schedule had put too much emphasis on "internal alignment" (equalizing pay for jobs that an evaluation procedure deems to be equal) and too little on external adjustment (paying rates comparable with those in the nonfederal sector). After reviewing some alternative restructurings of the white-

---

1. Results of this work appeared as the six-volume series, Studies of Federal White-Collar Compensation, several of which are cited below.

TABLE 4-1. *The Civil Service Commission's Proposed Division of the General Schedule into Four Occupational Services*

Occupational service	Number of employees	Percent of work force
Clerical and technician	563,793	39.9
Office clerical	455,155	. . .
Technician	108,638	. . .
Professional and administrative	744,904	52.7
Professional	197,926	. . .
Administrative	261,862	. . .
Government program execution	220,320	. . .
Technical	64,796	. . .
Executive and managerial	24,023	1.7
GS-16 to GS-18	6,787	. . .
GS-14 to GS-16	17,236	. . .
Special schedule	81,920	5.8
Protective services	36,240	. . .
Medical	10,296	. . .
Legal	12,712	. . .
Education	22,672	. . .
Total	1,414,640	100.0

Source: Civil Service Commission, Bureau of Policies and Standards, "Redesigning the General Schedule," Studies of Federal White-Collar Compensation, CPG 76-2 (CSC, October 1975), pp. 59–69. Figures are rounded.

collar work force, the commission recommended that the jobs covered at that time by the general schedule be split into four separate services, each with its own pay system and job evaluation plan to determine grades within each service. The four services (table 4-1) would be clerical and technician (with 40 percent of the work force); professional and administrative (53 percent); executive and managerial (2 percent); and special schedule (6 percent). The main reason for splitting the bulk of the general schedule into separate professional and clerical groups was to avoid the underpayment-overpayment problems in the GS-5–7 levels caused by averaging private sector salaries (as discussed in chapter 2).[2] In addition, the commission argued that there was enough evidence to show that the private sector pays different rates in different local labor markets for clerical and technician jobs; it therefore recommended that salaries for the clerical and technician service be based on local pay surveys.[3] The

2. Civil Service Commission, Bureau of Policies and Standards, "Redesigning the General Schedule," Studies of Federal White-Collar Compensation, CPG 76-2 (CSC, October 1975).

3. CSC, Bureau of Policies and Standards, "Locality Pay Study," Studies of Federal White-Collar Compensation, CPG 76-3 (CSC, October 1975).

other services would continue to have nationwide salaries. Finally, the commission endorsed the concept of total compensation comparability (pay plus fringes equalized in the federal and nonfederal sectors) but did not specify whether this was to mean equalizing pay and equalizing fringes separately but simultaneously or equalizing the sum of the two regardless of the composition of the parts.[4]

PRESIDENT'S PANEL ON FEDERAL COMPENSATION. In December 1975 this panel, better known as the Rockefeller Panel, delivered its report to President Ford.[5] The panel, which had been formed only six months earlier, relied heavily on the Civil Service Commission study. The Rockefeller Panel, however, changed some of the emphasis in its recommendations. First place went to endorsing total compensation comparability as the standard for federal compensation, although the panel did not take a stand on how to implement it.[6] The panel also strongly endorsed splitting the general schedule into a clerical and technical service and a professional, administrative, managerial, and executive service, with the former being paid on a local basis and the latter on a nationwide basis. Clerical workers who would lose pay if locality pay was implemented would be protected—the switch would be made gradually. The panel also recommended that pay surveys include matched jobs in state and local government (and private nonprofit organizations) "whenever necessary to obtain adequate samples and appropriate job matches."[7]

THE CARTER TASK FORCE. The election of a Democrat to the presidency initially made little difference in the civil service pay reform proposals. President Carter's Federal Personnel Management Project issued its report in December 1977.[8] It also endorsed total compensation comparability, splitting the general schedule, establishing locality pay for clerical and technical workers, and including state-local government workers in the comparability survey. Certain refinements were added to the findings of the previous reports.

The report said, "The long-term goal should be to move toward a

4. CSC, Bureau of Policies and Standards, "Total Compensation Comparability," Studies of Federal White-Collar Compensation, CPG 76-5 (CSC, October 1975), especially pp. 23ff.

5. *Report to the President of the President's Panel on Federal Compensation* (Government Printing Office, 1975).

6. Ibid., p. 7.

7. Ibid., p. 22.

8. "Personnel Management Project," vol. 1, "Final Staff Report" (President's Reorganization Project, 1977).

practice of Federal pay equal to non-Federal pay and each Federal benefit equal to each non-Federal benefit, except where there is a deliberate and demonstrated need for a variation."[9] In the short run, however, the report called for flexibility in establishing total compensation comparability.

The task force also strongly endorsed the principle of local pay rates for all white-collar workers, and supported national pay rates for professional and administrative workers only because of the "many potential problems [that] would surround the gathering of outside pay data for various professional and administrative levels by locality."[10] Foreshadowing political problems to come, the report noted that to implement local-rate pay for clerical and technical workers will have a mixed effect: "About 400,000 clerical and technical employees located in high-paying areas will get more pay under a local rate system; but another estimated 300,000 employees in lower-paying areas will be better off if the change is not made."[11]

Finally, the Carter task force took a stronger stand about adding state and local government employees to the comparability survey, arguing that the matched public employee jobs should be included, "in the same manner as the private sector."[12] The principal reason given was that state and local government salaries could no longer be considered "administered" rates, because those employees were being rapidly unionized. "Because of this . . . state and local pay rates have become increasingly more competitive."[13]

FIFTH ADVISORY COUNCIL ON SOCIAL SECURITY. In 1979 the advisory council presented a particularly comprehensive review of the social security system and related retirement issues. With respect to federal employees, the council advanced three major recommendations. First, it recommended that coverage under social security be mandatory for newly hired federal workers, citing as primary reasons gaps in coverage that now occur for workers who move between covered and uncovered employment and windfall benefits that accrue to federal employees who also qualify for social security after a short period in the private sector. Second, the council supported a plan for optional coverage under social

9. Ibid., p. 152.
10. Ibid., p. 158.
11. Ibid., p. 159.
12. Ibid.
13. Ibid., p. 156.

security for existing employees. Third, since universal coverage would take some time to implement, the council supported the institution of plans to coordinate civil service and social security benefits so that the windfall accruing to dual beneficiaries would be reduced or eliminated. On the crucial issue of how social security benefits should be supplemented for federal workers, the council commented that "it is our expectation that the combined protection of social security and the supplementary plans, with few exceptions, would provide protection as good as, or better than, that now provided by the staff plans alone."[14]

UNIVERSAL SOCIAL SECURITY COVERAGE STUDY GROUP. In March 1980 the study group issued a report on the "feasibility and desirability" of extending social security coverage to currently exempted employees. While the report avoids advocating any particular plan for covering federal employees under social security, it nonetheless clarifies many of the issues. The report demonstrates that if federal employees are covered by social security, there is no supplementary pension plan based on final salary and years of service that can entirely replicate (in combination with social security) the current civil service retirement system. Consequently, any supplementary plan that retains the basic structure of the CSR plan must be "targeted" on an employee with an assumed length of career, marital status, retirement year, and income level. In the report, therefore, attention is focused on a federal supplementary retirement system that in combination with social security would yield the same replacement rate as the current CSR program for a single worker retiring at age sixty-two with forty-two years of service and a final salary of $20,000. Such a program would simply modify the present CSR by lowering the rate at which each year of service raises the annuity to 1.15 percent of the high-3 average salary. The combined cost to the government of this plan and social security is about 2 percent of payroll below the cost of the current CSR system. The study group report shows that the plan would generate larger benefits than the current CSR system for workers with salaries below $20,000 but much smaller benefits for those with incomes above that level, mainly because the supplementary plan was not designed to offset the tilt in the social security benefit structure. The report suggests that a "thrift (savings) plan approach" might be used by employees whose combined benefits would be lowered by the

14. *Report of the 1979 Advisory Council on Social Security,* Committee Print, House Committee on Ways and Means, 96 Cong. 1 sess. (GPO, 1980), p. 166; see also pp. 161–71.

social security plus supplementary pension plan. The specific thrift plan analyzed (developed by the Office of Personnel and Management) would allow employees to set aside up to 6 percent of salary, with the federal government (as employer) matching each dollar saved with a fifty-cent contribution. The report estimates that this feature would cost the government between 1 and 2 percent of payroll (not incidentally bringing the total cost almost exactly up to that of the current CSR system). In sum, without advocating it, the study group made clear that universal coverage of federal employees under social security would be desirable (for the same reasons cited by the advisory council) and that at no additional cost to the government a supplementary plan with CSR characteristics could be implemented together with a thrift plan.[15]

The study group report also discusses alternative transition options for covering employees under social security. These range from covering only new hires and exempting all current employees to covering all future services of all current (and future) employees and exempting only those already eligible for civil service retirement. Intermediate options include various age and service combinations that could be used to determine who would be exempt from coverage. The study group found that the options that would allow large numbers of current employees to remain under the old system would only very slowly eliminate the windfall benefits available to dual beneficiaries (and might, therefore, require a more immediate plan to limit windfalls), whereas the options that would immediately cover all or most future service would be administratively complex (past service under CSR would have to be credited in social security) and might create some new windfalls.[16]

THE PRESIDENT'S PENSION COMMISSION. The President's Commission on Pension Policy issued its final report in February 1981.[17] Even though the commission took a strong stand on retirement age under social security (raised to age sixty-eight between the years 1990 and 2002) and on the desirability of supplementing pensions in the private sector (advocating a mandatory universal pension system funded at 3 percent

15. Department of Health, Education, and Welfare, Universal Social Security Coverage Study Group, "Report: The Desirability and Feasibility of Social Security Coverage for Employees of Federal, State and Local Governments and Private Non Profit Organizations" (March 1980), pp. 99–134.

16. Ibid.

17. President's Commission on Pension Policy, *Coming of Age: Toward a National Retirement Income Policy* (GPO, 1981).

of payroll), its report is timid in its recommendations for federal employees. The commission recommended extending social security coverage only to new workers in the federal (and state-local) government. Accordingly, it also favored immediate steps to eliminate coverage gaps and "unintended subsidies" for existing workers. The report makes no reference to the retirement age for federal workers or to the design of any supplementary civil service pension.

Legislative Proposals

The Carter administration not only initiated or received an unprecedented number of studies of the civil service system, it also sponsored the broadest reform legislation governing federal employees in decades. In 1978 the Civil Service Reform Act was passed. This law established a Senior Executive Service, established merit pay for certain categories of employees, and clarified issues relating to job transfer and removal from service. The act did not, however, deal with fundamental pay or benefit issues for the bulk of federal employees. These issues were taken up in subsequent proposals by both the Carter and the Reagan administrations.

The Federal Employees Compensation Reform Act of 1979

In 1979 President Carter proposed the Federal Employees Compensation Reform Act, which embodies almost all the pay reforms suggested in the earlier studies. The centerpiece of the legislation is its endorsement of the principle of total compensation comparability. "It is the policy of Congress that the total compensation of Federal employees . . . be fixed and adjusted from time to time in a manner consistent with the public interest based on the principles that: (1) Federal total compensation be comparable with non-Federal total compensation. . . . The purpose of the Federal compensation program is to provide total compensation which is adequate for recruiting, retaining, and managing a well-qualified workforce."[18]

The term "non-Federal" replaces "private enterprise" in the existing statutes to permit broadening the scope of the Bureau of Labor Statistics

18. Federal Employees Compensation Reform Act of 1979, sect. 5301 (H.R. 4487).

survey to include state and local government employees' compensation. In addition, the legislation provided that general schedule workers be paid on the basis of local pay schedules. Higher-level professional administrators within the general schedule (and all the Senior Executive Service and executive schedule work force) would be exempt from this provision and would continue to be paid on a uniform nationwide basis. Employees whose salary would drop under locality pay would be protected: they would retain their old pay but be granted partial salary increases until the locality pay rate caught up.

The 1979 Carter proposal omits one key feature of the reform agenda outlined in the reports reviewed in the last section: no mention is made of splitting the general schedule into the more homogeneous occupational groups of clerical and technical, and professional and administrative. Instead, the act proposes two alternative forms of pay flexibility. One would broaden the government's ability to establish "special occupational services" whenever the Office of Personnel Management determines that the "Government would be significantly handicapped in recruiting a well-qualified workforce" if that occupation was included in the general schedule. The special occupational service would have its own, higher pay schedule. In addition, the reform act establishes "staffing differentials," essentially a bonus system, to be used in individual cases or on the occupational or geographical basis that is pertinent to the government's hiring or retention problem.

The 1979 proposal also departs from previous task force reports by taking a strong stand on which element of compensation should be adjusted to attain total compensation comparability. It gives the president the authority to adjust benefits, "except those related to retirement," to fulfill the goals of the legislation. (A joint resolution of Congress may overturn a decision if the president accedes; otherwise two-thirds of each House of Congress would be needed.)[19] But the legislation also states that for five years after the date of enactment "there will be no downward adjustment" of those benefits that the act places under presidential discretion.[20] What these provisions amount to is the following: if the total compensation comparability survey indicates a reduced rate of compensation, the adjustment will be made in *salary rates,* at least for the first five years. In principle, a president could recommend

19. Ibid., sect. 5309.
20. Ibid., sect. 8.

legislation to restrain retirement benefits, but the proposal clearly signals the intent to concentrate the adjustment on salaries. Salary adjustment affects budget outlays immediately; most adjustments in civil service retirement would not bear budgetary fruit for many years.

Although President Carter's reform legislation was not enacted, his administration used the pay reform proposal to justify holding down salary increases in the budgets submitted in 1980 and 1981. These proposed budgetary savings from pay reform (using total compensation comparability rather than pay comparability) were about one-quarter of all the savings claimed by the administration in 1980, and were much larger than the savings from a proposal (eventually enacted) to reduce the frequency of indexing retirement programs, even though the latter proposal attracted much more public attention.[21]

How Total Compensation Comparability Was Attained

The pay restraints imposed by the Carter administration for its reform proposal were not based on actual data comparing the nonsalary benefits of the federal and private sectors. These data became available only in 1981, when the tabulation was completed for a special 1979 benefits survey conducted by the Bureau of Labor Statistics at the request of the Office of Personnel Management. The survey results, which are applicable to the March 1980 comparison of federal and private sector average pay rates, are shown in table 4-2.[22]

The results of the survey, shown in the upper part of the table, indicate that the sharply higher value of federal retirement benefits and disability insurance almost offsets the salary advantage of the average private sector worker. The comparison of sectors is little affected by the two other surveyed benefits, life and health insurance, which differ only by about 1 percent of payroll in the two sectors.[23] If these had been the only nonsalary benefits used, the average federal pay increase in 1980 under a total compensation standard would have been about 4 percent.

21. The budgetary savings included the effects of proposed reform in blue-collar pay as well as the total compensation comparability plan.

22. Office of Personnel Management, Compensation Group, "Total Compensation Comparability: Background, Method, Preliminary Results" (OPM, July 1981), pp. 18–19. The survey did not encompass state and local governments in either pay or benefits. No such survey has yet been taken.

23. Differences in hours worked, including the effect of holidays and leave, amount to a less than 1 percent difference as well. See ibid.

TABLE 4-2. *Salary and Nonsalary Benefits of the Average Worker in the Federal and Private Sectors, March 1980*[a]

	Federal sector		Private sector	
Compensation component	Amount (dollars)	Percent of salary	Amount (dollars)	Percent of salary
Salary	19,906	. . .	22,587	. . .
Retirement and disability	5,613	28.2	3,772	16.7
Life insurance	60	0.3	113	0.5
Health insurance	760	3.8	1,045	4.6
Survey-based total	26,339	. . .	27,517	. . .
Secondary benefits	239	1.2	1,446	6.4
Leave-adjustment factor	. . .	. . .	− 294	− 1.3
Total	26,578	. . .	28,669	. . .

Source: Office of Personnel Management, Compensation Group, "Total Compensation Comparability: Background, Method, Preliminary Results" (OPM, July 1981), pp. 18–19.
a. Salary data for March 1980. Fringe benefits as a percent of salary based on 1979 survey data.

The OPM, however, also includes the value of a wide variety of other benefits, which are derived from "published sources," in estimating total compensation. These secondary benefits are profit sharing, parking, bonuses, severance pay, miscellaneous paid nonwork time, and the like. For these benefits, the private sector is found to be much more generous than the federal government.[24] As a result, when the OPM estimated the pay raise for 1980 to achieve total compensation comparability, the required average percentage increase was 8.8 percent.[25] Since the actual pay increase in October 1980 was 9.1 percent, it follows that total compensation comparability was almost exactly realized in that year. Had the Reagan administration accepted this result, it could have argued that all future pay raises between sectors should be equalized.[26]

24. It is less generous with regard to unpaid time off, however, so this is counted as a negative fringe benefit—the leave-adjustment factor in table 4-3.
25. OPM, Compensation Group, "Total Compensation Comparability." The OPM does not adjust for the time lag in pay discussed in chapter 2.
26. Once total compensation comparability is attained by adjusting federal salaries for superior federal fringe benefits, the total compensation standard would call for equal percent increases in salary between sectors unless (or until) the ratio of fringe benefits to pay changes. Thus if private sector fringes are always 15 percent of salary (say $15 and $100 initially) and federal fringes are always 30 percent of salary ($26.50 and $88.50 for total comparability) and the private sector salary rises by 10 percent (to $110), a federal pay raise of 10 percent (to a salary of $97.40) will restore total compensation comparability.

Comparability Lost: President Reagan's Plan

In most regards President Reagan's initial pay reform proposal resembled President Carter's. The Federal Pay Comparability Reform Act of 1981 retains the single general schedule for all white-collar occupations and endorses locality pay and the surveying of compensation in state and local governments.[27] It proposes to achieve some pay flexibility by "special rates of pay" for any labor market segment where the government is having "difficulty in recruiting or retaining well-qualified individuals." For workers whose pay might be cut under any provision of the legislation, a minimum of a 2 percent yearly pay raise is guaranteed for the first five years.

The most significant departure in President Reagan's proposal was to promulgate a new standard for federal total compensation, to be equal to 94 percent of nonfederal total compensation, "thereby recognizing those aspects of Federal employment which make it more attractive than many comparably-paid jobs in the private sector."[28] The attractive aspects of federal employment cited by the Office of Personnel Management include "such factors as job security, promotion potential, portability of benefits, etc." There was no analysis of why these factors add up to about 6 percent of pay. It is perhaps no coincidence that the secondary benefits advantage of the private sector reported by OPM was in that range. The 94 percent standard eliminates the effect of counting these secondary benefits.[29]

The effect of the Reagan administration's proposed 94 percent compensation standard was to justify holding down federal salary increases due in October 1981, 1982, and 1983. A comparison of this

27. Introduced March 31, 1981, as S.838.
28. "Budget Reform Plan," press release, Office of the President, February 18, 1981, p. 8-6.
29. The Reagan administration's pay reform proposal modified the Carter plan in one other important respect. Unlike the Carter plan, which called for measuring only the average value of nonsalary benefits, the Reagan bill calls for the comparability measure to be made for "the same levels of work" (S.838, sect. 5301). This provision, which would invalidate a major objection to the Carter proposal (see next section), cannot at present be implemented, because the OPM has no methodology to allocate the value of benefits to particular classes of employees. In using the 94 percent standard to justify pay-raise proposals, the Reagan administration has employed only the estimated average value of benefits.

TABLE 4-3. *Projected Federal Pay Raises under Three Standards, 1981–84*

Percent

Year	Assumed private sector salary increase	Current law	100 percent total compen-sation com-parability	94 percent total compensation comparability (phased in)[a]
1981	9.1	15.1	8.6	4.8
1982	8.9	8.9	8.9	7.0
1983	7.9	7.9	7.9	7.0
1984	7.0	7.0	7.0	7.0

Source: Office of Management and Budget, *Budget Revisions, Fiscal Year 1982* (GPO, 1981). Assumed private sector salary increases are noted in source as "Federal Pay Raise, Military."
a. The Reagan administration's proposal.

proposal with current law and with 100 percent total compensation comparability is given in table 4-3. Had the 94 percent standard been implemented immediately, the federal pay raise in 1981 would have been 2.1 percent.[30] President Reagan, however, decided to phase in implementation of that standard and proposed a 4.8 percent pay increase for 1981. The "excess" of 2.7 percentage points was to be removed over the next two years; with the 1983 pay raise, the 94 percent standard was to be met.[31]

Criticism of the Pay Reform Legislation

The main objections to the Carter-Reagan reform package—the first two items that follow—pertain to what it has already done and what it does not propose to do. The details of the legislation itself are less objectionable, although many unresolved questions have never been satisfactorily answered by the proponents.

SALARY HOLD-DOWNS. The proposal for total compensation comparability affected government policy even though it was never passed. It was used by both the Carter and Reagan administrations as an excuse or

30. Full total compensation comparability would have raised the average federal salary in 1981 to 108.6 percent of its level in 1980 (table 4-3). Ninety-four percent of this level is 102.08, or 2.1 percent above the 1980 average salary.

31. In early 1982 President Reagan withdrew his pay reform legislation and abandoned its principles as the rationale for federal pay raises. His fiscal 1983 budget arbitrarily called for 5 percent annual raises in 1982, 1983, and 1984. Congress and the administration finally agreed to a 4 percent raise for 1982.

rationale for successive across-the-board hold-downs of federal employee salary increases. These limits on federal pay raises are the main
reason why salary rates in the upper parts of the general schedule are so
out of line with salary rates in the private sector. That the same employees
are also the primary beneficiaries of the overgenerous civil service
retirement system is comforting in only the narrowest sense. As long as
the retirement program remains as it is, holding down the salary of
advanced career professionals and managers will be a tempting goal for
any budget-conscious president or Congress. Moreover, the combination of generous retirement and undernourished payroll encourages
retirement from government at an early age, depriving the government of the services of its most experienced workers. Thus attaining
total compensation comparability in either its 100 percent or 94 percent
form is no solution to serious problems besetting federal personnel
policy.

NO GENERAL SCHEDULE REFORM. The omission from the reform legislation of the proposal by the Rockefeller Panel and others to split the
general schedule is another large defect. In the middle grades of the
general schedule, the use of a single rate of pay to cover both clerical
and professional and administrative employees guarantees that the
former will be overpaid and the latter underpaid relative to the private
market. Although overpayment of salary to some clerical workers can
be viewed as compensation for their being deprived of participation in
social security—a retirement program tilted in favor of relatively low-
paid workers—it is constantly cited as proof of government's over-
generosity. Moreover, the low salaries paid to entry-level professionals
because of the common pay schedule for all occupations probably leads
to overpromotion and overgrading of jobs, thus distorting the entire
federal pay structure. No federal pay reform program can be complete
without dealing with this crucial source of malfunction in current federal
pay practice.

USE OF LOCAL PAY SCALES. The proposal to compensate federal employees according to pay scales in local labor markets is obviously
desirable in principle. The original proposal called for local pay only for
clerical and technical workers, a relatively narrow occupational group-
ing for which government surveys could probably identify high-wage
and low-wage markets. But the Carter-Reagan pay package proposes to
apply a single regional differential for each grade that is applicable to all
workers in that grade. This proposal implicitly assumes that regional

differences are uniform across occupations. For example, if private sector pay rates in Atlanta are 90 percent of the national average for both clerical and professional workers at GS-5, a single pay differential would unambiguously improve federal pay practice. If, however, regional variations in pay are different for various occupations, the proposed single regional adjustment could actually worsen the rationality of the federal pay system. For instance, if Atlanta's pay rate is 85 percent of the national average for clerical workers but 105 percent for professionals, an Atlanta differential of 95 will make it more difficult to recruit professionals there than if the pay was based on national averages. At present no data set exists that can throw much light on this question of uniformity of pay relative to occupation.[32] Until such data are collected and analyzed it would seem premature to accept locality pay scales.[33]

INCLUSION OF STATE AND LOCAL GOVERNMENTS. The pay reform proposal to include state and local governments in the universe against which comparability is measured may also prove a mixed blessing. The possibility of expanding the number of matched jobs in the annual survey, and of improving the match for currently surveyed jobs, should be significantly strengthened by surveying state and local governments. Everyone would have more confidence in salary data for the job title "personnel director" if the federal jobs in this category were being compared with jobs in the state governments of Michigan, California, and New York as well as with those in manufacturing and utilities corporations. With fringe benefits, however, the inclusion of state and local governments in the survey poses some problems. Studies of state-local government pension programs have found a large number of them to be overgenerous (relative to the likely willingness of taxpayers to pay the bills) and to be seriously underfunded. As a result, many governments are currently scaling back their pension promises (and improving the soundness of the funding systems). It does not make sense for the federal government's survey of retirement benefits in the nonfederal sector to include plans that are known to be unrealistic. (And it makes even less

32. For an analysis of data covering primarily clerical jobs, see CSC, Bureau of Policies and Standards, "Locality Pay Study." See Congressional Budget Office, *Compensation Reform for Federal White-Collar Employees: The Administration's Proposal and Budget Options for 1981* (GPO, 1980), pp. 8–11, for an attempt to use census data for this comparison.

33. Another problem that needs to be thought through before implementing locality pay is how to deal with the Washington, D.C., market. Because federal employment dominates in this market, private sector pay is not independently arrived at.

sense to include the unrealistic plans in one year's survey and the scaled-down plan the next year, thereby lowering and then raising comparable federal compensation.) On balance, including state and local governments in the universe for the comparability survey appears to be a constructive proposal, but initially the data should be presented both with and without the effects of inclusion so that any anomalies arising from retirement programs can be easily identified.

SPECIAL PAY RATES. Both the Carter and Reagan reform plans attempt to introduce more flexibility into the pay system by establishing special pay rates in cases where the government is having difficulty in recruiting and retaining a qualified work force. In principle, this kind of flexibility could be used to turn around the traditional rigid civil service pay system completely. That is, the government could operate on a tight *overall* standard of compensation (for example, 78 percent of nonfederal compensation) and selectively designate various occupations or geographical areas to be special cases. The result would be a lower overall wage bill, since the money for above-minimum salaries would be used only where it was needed to solve a work-force problem.

However attractive such an approach to setting pay may appear, it is probably unworkable for the federal government on at least three grounds. First, the analytical capability to monitor and enforce market-based differential wage systems would greatly outstrip current staff capacity. Since virtually every subagency manager would want to claim that his office needed special rates of pay to maintain a quality work force, a rigorous independent means of adjudicating such claims would be necessary. This would require the collection of data on work-force quality, quit rates, and retirement rates and the construction of models to determine the legitimacy of claims—a big order for a work force as numerous and diversified as the federal government's.

Second, a broad system of diversified pay with a large number of exceptions to the basic pay schedule could become a disadvantage in recruiting for government service. Private sector corporations often maintain complex pay differentials for different areas of job skills; in the public sector, however, such differentials would have to be explicit, on paper, inflexible, and subject to review and appeal. (Taxpayers' money always deserves tight rules, since there is no market check on its expenditure.) This means a forbiddingly complex answer to the young recruit's favorite question, "What would I be paid?" Even the present civil service compensation structure of grades and steps and retirement credits is incredibly complicated; multiple rates might make the system administratively unmanageable.

Third, more than private sector pay systems, the civil service needs to be thought of as "fair" and free of political or capricious actions. The current system of a common pay schedule with few exceptions (such as physicians, who do receive higher rates of pay) is perhaps a too pure version of the classic civil service ethic. But if "personnel directors" or "the president's hometown" were declared labor market categories in need of special rates of pay, the underlying spirit of fairness could break down. The loss of esprit de corps and of basic honesty among federal employees, which stem in large part from the feeling of a politics-free civil service, would be a large loss indeed.

For these reasons it is probably desirable that the request for broader authority for special rates of pay be limited. Congress should want to specify fairly rigid controls and reporting requirements on any such exercise of authority to ensure that special rates are used only in ways that do not undermine the basic features of the current pay system. In this regard, one innovation not proposed in the Carter or Reagan reform plan would introduce some symmetry into the special rates system. Specifically, the language of the legislation could be modified to allow the government in limited cases to rule that an occupation or a geographical area had an excess labor supply and warranted special (in this case, lower) rates of pay. Such a balanced approach to flexibility would give any government finding of imbalance in labor markets the appearance of fairness (because there would be some findings on either side); it would constrain the use of special rates (because the government officials in charge of the program would seek a balanced approach); and it would counter the notion that special rates are a means of showing favoritism to some groups. If such a symmetrical special rate system was implemented, it could be used as a way to ease into locality pay rates without committing the government to national implementation from the start.

OBJECTIVITY OF STANDARDS. Any quantitative assessment of total compensation comparability between the federal and nonfederal sectors will be driven by the estimated value of the retirement plans in the two sectors. At several points in this book I have indicated that many problematic assumptions must be made in order to evaluate the employer's costs of retirement, such as assumptions about the economy and about the incidence of future social security liabilities. As noted in appendix B, these assumptions can affect the estimated costs of retirement (and the gaps between sectors) significantly. Here three additional points need to be made.

First, whatever economic assumptions are initially used to evaluate future retirement benefits, they will almost certainly need to be revised in the future, if past history is any guide. The timing and extent of such revisions are not objectively predetermined events. There is no magic moment when the assumption of an x percent inflation rate becomes unrealistic. Therefore, an administration that sought to restrain federal outlays in any given year would probably choose that year to officially revise some of the unknowable economic assumptions (in the right direction). Under the current salary comparability rules, at least, an "objective" pay standard exists. To be sure, that standard is frequently circumvented, but only after the president makes his case for an alternative plan. Under the total compensation comparability standard, the problematic nature of the assumptions needed to estimate the retirement benefit value and the probable need for periodic revisions would inevitably make the standard itself appear less objective and more political.

Second, the difference between the degree of indexation of retirement benefits in the federal and private sectors poses another challenge to objective measurement. Part of the value of complete indexation, as in civil service retirement, is that it provides the beneficiary with insurance against unanticipated inflation. None of the methods for comparing compensation in the two sectors explicitly tries to evaluate this insurance component. Indeed, it would be impossible to evaluate it now, because no market exists for such insurance. The absence of empirical evidence about such an important component of compensation invites arbitrary evaluations, driven more by budgetary needs or assessment of the public's resentment over federal retirees' benefits than by honest labor market evaluations.

Third, the choice between an objective standard that seems impossible to achieve and a fuzzy, manipulable standard that might possibly be attained is not an easy one. Such standards as the fifty-five-mile-an-hour highway speed limit, the requirements of the Clean Air Act, or even dog leashing statutes are a case in point. An attractive compromise for federal compensation would be to require the president to issue a full report whenever a significant change is made in the computation of benefits, to have that report reviewed by an outside group such as the Advisory Committee on Federal Pay,[34] and to require congressional approval wherever the outside committee finds fault with the procedures. Such a process would increase the chance that the total compensation standard would be viewed as objective. President Carter's legislative proposal included the requirement for a report and for review, but not for explicit congressional approval of a change. President Reagan's proposal was mute on review procedures.

MEASUREMENT AND ADJUSTMENT OF COMPENSATION. Two final issues are raised by the pay reform legislation: should the value of the benefit component be computed by grade or only in the aggregate, and should the finding of a lack of comparability in one component of compensation be permitted to occasion an offsetting adjustment in another component?

The economic logic of total compensation comparability suggests that compensation be measured and adjusted by grade or occupation, or both, and not simply by an average. Suppose, for example, that after total compensation comparability has been in place for some years, tax laws pertaining to health insurance benefits are changed; as a result, private sector employers restructure their health insurance benefits so that their value to low-paid employees (say, clerical workers) is greatly reduced and the value to high-paid workers (say, managers) is increased. Suppose that on average there is no change in the overall value of private sector health benefits and that private sector salaries are not adjusted at all. This implies a shift in relative compensation in the private sector toward higher-paid workers. If a purpose of total compensation comparability is to enhance the public sector's competitiveness in labor markets, the government would need to raise the compensation of the higher grades and lower that of lower grades even though average total compensation comparability has not changed. Only by such a restructuring of relative compensation could the government maintain its attractiveness to managers and avoid paying an unnecessary bonus to its clerical staff, whose private sector counterparts have had their compensation reduced.

It would make sense to use the average value of benefits in each sector as the sole measurement in determining comparability only if benefits had the same ratio to salary at all salary levels. Under all other

34. The advisory committee is a group of experts from the private sector whose current role is to review the report of the president's pay agent and advise the president on procedures and findings.

circumstances, total compensation must be measured according to grade and adjustments to compensation must be based on grade-by-grade estimates if the goals of government labor-market competitiveness and avoidance of waste are to be achieved. President Carter's reform proposal did not require grade-by-grade measurement; neither the Carter nor Reagan administration ever invoked any concept of total compensation other than the average difference between sectors; and the Office of Personnel Management's comparability methodology calculates only an average value of benefits.

As for the second issue, suppose nonsalary benefits were uniformly higher for federal employees than for their nonfederal counterparts. Is it wise for the government to make up for such incomparability in benefits by an equivalent reduction in salary? This question will obviously be at the heart of debates over total compensation comparability as long as federal retirement benefits remain so much ahead of those in the private sector.

The case for trading off one element of compensation (lower salary) for another (higher retirement) has to be based on one of two arguments. First, if it can be demonstrated that by altering the composition of the compensation package commonly found in the private sector, the government can attract a work force with more desirable characteristics for each compensation dollar spent, then an efficiency case for trading salary for fringes can be made. Under present conditions, it would have to be proved that the people who are drawn into government by a low salary–high (and indexed) retirement pay structure are somehow better suited to government service than others. One can only guess at the kind of person who would be attracted by such a package: a person who applies a relatively low discount rate to future income, who has relatively good access to capital markets or to sources of income other than his own wages, and who is pessimistic about the prospects of curbing inflation and, therefore, will give up a lot of current salary for a fully indexed retirement. To my knowledge, it has never been demonstrated that it would be desirable to entice into public service people with these characteristics.[35]

35. It has been argued that the government is acting rationally by maximizing retirement and minimizing pay, because its high-earning work force has the most to gain from avoiding taxes on salary. This is wrong. If the comparison of benefits is made for similar jobs, then the question is, why should the government take more advantage of tax shelters than the private sector does in compensating a grade 14 economist? If

Second, the case can be made that on political grounds it is more difficult to adjust some elements of compensation than others and that it is better to make the adjustment where it is feasible than to do nothing at all. This certainly must have been part of the rationale for the Carter-Reagan hold-downs of salary: that was feasible, whereas cutting retirement benefits (the source of the government workers' advantage) was not.

The counterargument is, first of all, that a significant imbalance between sectors in any element of total compensation presumably indicates that something is amiss in that element and should be corrected. It is always risky to correct one element of compensation for an imbalance in another because the estimator's valuation of one element's excess may seriously miss the potential employee's valuation. Thus item-by-item comparability, which is much easier to measure and adjust for, ought to be the preferred solution.

Because the federal government is the nation's largest employer, the various components of its compensation package are the object of intense interest by unions and other employee groups. The interest is generally asymmetric: interest is high in generous benefits and negligible in skimpy aspects of federal compensation. Thus, as far as federal compensation serves as a model for private sector labor bargains, a federal policy of keeping some aspects of compensation comparatively high will create pressure in the private sector to match those aspects.

For example, many labor groups in the nonfederal sector view the civil service's provision for relatively early retirement at full pension as a goal for them. The fact that federal civil service salaries or life insurance is kept low to pay for the liberal retirement age would not help management at the bargaining table. Inevitably any component of compensation that is much more generous in the federal than in the private sector will be interpreted as "federal policy," or at least as a legitimate goal for private sector negotiators to pursue. Moreover, as long as such a gap favoring federal employees persists, it maintains a climate of public resentment that can be exploited by any administration or Congress seeking quick budgetary savings. Specifically, as long as the public knows that federal employees can retire early at a fully indexed full

---

the government does so, the economists it gains are lost to the private sector. Thus only if the government attracts the "right" GS-14 economist from the pool by offering more retirement benefits is there an efficiency gain.

pension and easily qualify for social security as well, a shortsighted
president can gain public support for virtually any hold-down in salary,
even for one well beyond the requirements for total comparability.

These competing views of the merits of trading off one aspect of
federal compensation for another seem to lead in one policy direction:
the first priority in reforming federal compensation is to try to assess and
reform *each* element of the compensation. No major component of
compensation should be left in excess of private sector practice unless
the government wishes to signal a shortcoming in private sector practice.
After such a comprehensive reform is put into place—or after it fails—
then would be the right time to consider compensatory changes among
the elements of total compensation.[36]

Priorities for Reform: A Proposal

The pay reform proposals of Presidents Carter and Reagan avoid
grappling directly with the chief inadequacies of the current system for
setting and adjusting federal salaries, and they do not deal at all with
retirement reform. An alternative way to improve federal compensation
practices is to tackle the main problems directly through reform legislation. In this section, I set out one such program that would mean a sharp
break with past policies and may therefore be thought politically impossible. But the fact that a sharp deterioration in the quality of the federal
work force under present practices (or under total comparability
compensation reform in its salary-repressing form) could occur may
make radical reform more appealing than usual. In any event, prac-
tical legislators need a place to start, and I hope these proposals will
provide it.

Retirement Reform

As seen in chapter 3, the single most important decision facing the
government with respect to civil service retirement reform is whether
federal employees should be included in social security. The case for
coverage is impressive: elimination of windfall benefits to dual beneficiaries, elimination of the unjust sheltering of high-paid federal employ-

36. For a similar view see Advisory Committee on Federal Pay, "Eight Years of
Federal White-Collar Pay Comparability" (June 29, 1979).

ees from taxes used in a redistributive manner, better protection for low-paid employees, and the gain in public confidence in government from knowing that federal employees are in the same retirement boat as everyone else. Against these benefits from universal coverage, there are virtually no sound arguments. But there are transitional problems in moving to social security as well as concern about how social security would be supplemented.

THE HIGH-COST OPTION. A supplementary pension plan can be designed that would retain most of the characteristics of the current civil service retirement program. It would base supplementary retirement benefits on the high-3 salary and a (scaled-down) credit for years of service. Full retirement at the current early age and years combinations could be retained, with the employee taking some losses up to age sixty-two, when his social security benefit became available. Retirement benefits could continue to be indexed, and the plan could be integrated with social security so that all employees with incomes up to between $20,000 and $30,000 would be as well off as under the present civil service retirement plan.[37] The cost of such a supplementary program, combined with the government's cost as employer under social security, could be just as high as that of the present retirement system.

This high-cost option can be faulted on several grounds. Because it is just as expensive as the present program, it will continue to cause public resentment over coddled federal retirees—although elimination of dual beneficiaries will temper that resentment. Retaining the high-3 salary to determine retirement benefits would continue the current disincentive for mobility between the federal government and the private sector and could maintain the current incentive for retirement at the earliest age of eligibility (see chapter 3). The failure of such a retirement program to distinguish between the retirement needs of single and married persons (except insofar as social security makes that distinction) makes the proposal unnecessarily inflexible.

REFORM SUPPLEMENTARY RETIREMENT (RSR). It is possible to design a program to deal with all these problems. Under RSR, up to 18 percent of a federal employee's total earnings could be set aside in an individual retirement account (IRA). The government would contribute much more than the employee for the first 7 percent of salary saved, less than the

37. Such proposals are discussed in detail in HEW, Universal Social Security Coverage Study Group, "Report."

employee for the next 7 percent, and nothing for the last 4 percent. For example:

Fraction of salary contributed	Employee contribution	Employer contribution
Up to 7 percent	Up to 2 percent	Up to 5 percent
Next 7 percent	5 percent	2 percent
Next 4 percent	4 percent	0 percent
Total (18 percent)	11 percent	7 percent

The accumulations in the RSR-IRA accounts would be fully vested (belong to the employee) and their earnings would be tax-free. Withdrawals would be penalized as under ordinary IRAs. The employee would have the right to choose to place his account with any bank, savings institution, mutual fund, pension fund, or insurance company that offered RSR-IRAs. Some accounts would grow faster than wages, some less—the employee would be taking the risk.

To maintain the availability of an indexed retirement benefit, the federal government would promise at the employee's retirement to issue to the firm managing the account index bonds in maturities approximating the expected remaining lifetime of the retiree. The availability of such an investment would make it possible for the RSR-IRA fund manager to offer the retiree an indexed annuity.

ADVANTAGES OF RSR. The combined RSR and social security plan for federal retirees has many advantages over the CSR system and over social security combined with the costly modified CSR plan. The first advantage is the program's cost. The maximum amount the federal government would put into RSR accounts is 7 percent of payroll. (That level would be reached only if all employees chose to have a total of 11 percent of their salary set aside in RSR-IRAs each year—an unlikely possibility.) This cost is on a par with the 6.4 percent of payroll that the Office of Personnel Management estimates to be the normal cost of private pension plans (see chapter 3). Instituting this reform program would thus mean that for the chief nonsalary benefit—retirement—the federal and nonfederal worker would be receiving comparable treatment.

The program's second advantage is its flexibility in allowing employees to select the level of retirement benefits that is most likely to be adequate to their needs. For married and single workers at different

TABLE 4-4. *Replacement and Savings Rates Needed to Supplement Social Security Benefits for Single and Married Workers at Selected Salary Levels, 1980*

Salary in dollars; rates in percent

Salary	Replacement rate needed after social security to maintain full consumption[a]	Rate of savings needed to achieve replacement[b]
Single worker		
10,000	24	11
15,000	24	11
20,000	26	12
30,000	31	16
50,000	30	16
Married worker		
10,000	5	2
15,000	7	3
20,000	15	7
30,000	26	12
50,000	30	15

a. Figures from tables 3-9 and 3-10.
b. Assumes a thirty-five-year career, an annual real wage increase of 1 percent, and a real interest rate of 1 percent. Derivation given in chapter 3, note 23.

salary levels the savings needed to supplement social security to ensure maintenance of preretirement consumption levels vary greatly. As shown in table 4-4, a married worker with a $10,000 salary would have to set aside only 2 percent of annual income to build up a fund sufficient to raise retirement income to preretirement consumption levels,[38] while one with a $50,000 salary would need 15 percent. The RSR plan would fairly heavily subsidize the retirement needs of married workers up to $20,000, about the average employee, and offer less subsidy to the savings needs of higher earners. Workers in all salary-marital classes could achieve a full consumption replacement rate under the RSR plan.

The third advantage of the program is enhancement of job mobility for federal workers. Since the RSR is fully vested and is quasi-indexed during the employee's working career (in that the yield on fund investments is credited to the account), an employee does not give up anything if he leaves federal service in midcareer. And since he is already covered

38. Under RSR the worker would contribute 0.6 percent and the government 1.4 percent of salary to this total.

by social security, there would be no hiatus in establishing coverage under that program as there is under the present arrangements. Mobility into the government for people who take a short assignment would also be encouraged under this plan: all the funds in the RSR fund would belong to the worker, whereas the current CSR refunds only the employee's contribution (plus nominal interest of 3 percent if employment is between one and five years).

Mobility in the federal government is important for two reasons. One, total federal employment is not likely to grow in the foreseeable future. The only way to bring in "new blood" and accommodate needs for a changing mix of work skills in a stagnant work force is to allow people to move in and out with fewer impediments. Two, since federal workers do not have the right to strike, a good case can be made for allowing them to "vote with their feet." Under current CSR rules workers take too large a loss if they quit before retirement age; under RSR a resignation is much less costly, and it establishes the worker's effective right to voice his dissatisfaction by quitting his job.

The fourth advantage is that the RSR plan is fully funded. Unlike the current CSR plan, which is heavily subsidized by taxpayers when the benefits are paid (see chapter 3), the RSR funds itself after retirement is reached.[39] Moreover, during the accumulation period the RSR-IRA accounts would be a source of capital to private industry. Whether such a source would add to the net savings in the economy depends on how the government's saving (deficit or surplus) is affected and how the employee's saving is affected. On balance, one would expect some addition to total savings from the RSR plan.

POSSIBLE OBJECTIONS TO RSR. There are two elements of the program that will displease some workers. First, a primary source of savings to the government from the proposed plan would come from the deliberalizing of the retirement age implicit in the program. Workers would be subject to the same rules that govern social security and individual retirement accounts. Full pension from the former is available only at age sixty-five (with a reduced benefit available at age sixty-two), and one can avoid tax penalties on the latter only by postponing withdrawals

39. The government's only liability in retirement would be to pay the excess of interest on index bonds over and above what the interest would have been on nonindex bonds. This amount is a function of how the real interest rate on index bonds compares to market real interest rates. By setting a low real rate, the government could make this cost negligible.

until age fifty-nine and a half. Practically speaking, the institution of this program would sharply discourage federal employees from retiring before age sixty-two, whereas at present over 60 percent retire by that age (table 3-11). This change would obviously be viewed as a loss by those current employees who would be affected by it and by prospective employees, who could not look forward to retirement at an early age. From the government-as-employer's perspective, the deterrent to youthful retirement would be mixed news. While it would help retain key experienced personnel who are now driven into retirement by the CSR system, it would also prolong the working period for some employees who have outlived their usefulness.

Second, the proposed reform program would concentrate the losses squarely on the high-earning federal employee.[40] That is because the existing CSR program is so advantageous to such employees. Here is an idea of the magnitude of the loss to a $50,000 employee: under the current CSR system he can expect to receive retirement benefits sufficient to replace 110 percent of his preretirement standard of living (table 3-10) for an annual contribution of $3,500 (7 percent of pay). Under the proposed reform plan, if the worker contributed the maximum to the RSR plan (his 11 percent and the government's 7 percent), he could attain about 100 percent replacement, and the annual cost would be about $7,500 (about $2,000 to social security and $5,500 to RSR). Thus, to attain slightly less retirement income, the high-earning employee would have to more than double his contribution. The loss to lower-income employees would be much less and in some cases nonexistent, because of the social security tilt that benefits them.

TRANSITIONAL PROBLEMS. I have discussed losses and gains here as if the reform plan would be implemented in full, tomorrow. That of course cannot, and should not, happen. An employee who has served the government for twenty-nine years and is fifty-four years old cannot suddenly be told that the full pension he or she expects next year is postponed for seven years and is payable at a lower rate. That kind of change was overwhelmingly rejected by Congress when an attempt was made in 1981 to severely, and instantly, reduce social security benefits.[41] All transitional problems can be avoided if the reform retirement program is put in place only for new hires of the government, with existing

---

40. Including many of those who might draft the reform legislation.

41. For a summary of President Reagan's proposals to cut social security benefits, see *National Journal,* May 16, 1981, p. 867.

employees continuing under the CSR system. This approach has the disadvantage that the improvements gained by the reform system (lower cost, elimination of dual benefits, and so on) will be long in coming. In addition, if there was a large salary increase for upper-grade employees, which I propose in the next section, it would have to be reserved for new hires, creating a messy two-tier salary system. Of course, many in-between possibilities for a transition exist (for example, new hires plus employees under forty to be covered under the new plan). It is beyond the scope of this book to delve into these alternatives,[42] but my political hunch would be that a "new hires" approach is the only feasible one. This would mean that the "losses" in deliberalized retirement age and smaller replacement rates for currently employed high-earners would be paper losses. Even though the new hires approach would take a long time to bear fruit, its attractiveness is, I believe, so great that the wait would be worth it.[43]

Pay Reform

The heart of pay reform is to move strongly and boldly on three fronts: splitting the general schedule, instituting better controls over employment levels, and making a one-time salary adjustment (taken in conjunction with retirement reform) to eliminate the huge gaps that have developed in professional and managerial pay. It is also essential that retirement reform take place at the same time as pay reform.

TWO-PART GENERAL SCHEDULE. The advantages of splitting the general schedule have been discussed earlier. To review: in the private-sector jobs that are matched to the middle GS grades (5 and 7), clerical pay is much lower than professional and administrative pay. By setting one rate of pay for these grades, the government simultaneously overpays clerical workers and underpays entry-level professionals. This sets off a chain of rapid promotions and creative job upgradings to compensate the young professionals for the poor rates of pay. The result is a lack of integrity in the personnel process and a growing danger that the government will not attract quality entry-level professionals and managers. There is no way out of this impasse but to establish separate pay systems

42. See HEW, Universal Social Security Coverage Study Group, "Report," p. 134ff.

43. If universal coverage were started on a "new hires" basis, integration of benefits for dual beneficiaries probably should be implemented. See ibid.

for these two groups, as was recognized by all the panels whose reports were summarized earlier in the chapter.

The case against splitting the schedule is that the resulting clerical and technical service would disproportionately employ women and minorities. It is contended that the private-sector clerical salaries to which this service would be compared are artificially low because of the discrimination practiced in the private sector for these "women's jobs." But, as argued in chapter 2, such discrimination should not be a reason for distorting federal pay schedules. If discrimination is judged by Congress to be practiced in the private sector and if Congress wishes to prevent such unfairness in federal employment, then it can pass a law raising pay for the clerical and technical service by x percent. This would prevent private sector discrimination from being carried over to public sector employment, but still allow market-based determination of pay in the separate professional and managerial schedule.

BETTER PLANNING AND BUDGETARY CONTROLS. The artificial raising of grades that results from government agencies looking for ways to get around underpayment for professionals may at least help lure some able people into the government; the effect of the budget-and-slot-control system on grading, however, has no merit at all. As indicated in chapter 2, the current practice of allocating personnel limits to federal agencies tends to make managers hire relatively many high-grade employees. Because agencies are not effectively constrained by their budgets for salaries and expenses, but by slots, they hire the rich blend of inside workers and use the "leftover" salary and expense money for low-priority purchases, including consultants. All these practices directly or indirectly add to federal personnel costs and certainly do not contribute to an image of efficiency-in-government.

The General Accounting Office has repeatedly advocated eliminating all slot limits and replacing them with budget dollar controls. In a recent report the GAO comes close to advocating separate reporting and budgeting for consultants, noting that now it is virtually impossible to determine how much consulting costs and to what degree it is a subvention of personnel costs.[44] These proposals, if coupled with a tight reporting system that tracks agency employment and grade structure, give promise of a more rational management system than now exists.

44. See General Accounting Office, Comptroller General of the United States, *Improving the Credibility and Management of the Federal Work Force through Better Planning and Budgetary Controls*, FPCO-81-54 (GAO, 1981).

TABLE 4-5. *Full Pay Comparability in 1980 for Clerical and Technical Services and Professional and Administrative Services, Selected General Schedule Levels*
Dollars unless otherwise specified

GS level	March 1981 private sector pay rates		March 1980 federal pay rates	October 1980 pay raise needed for pay comparability with no time lag (percent)	
	Clerical and technical	Professional and administrative		Clerical and technical	Professional and administrative
1	8,687	. . .	7,122	22	. . .
3	12,526	. . .	9,551	31	. . .
4	13,734	. . .	11,148	23	. . .
5	14,715	16,944	12,733	16	33
6	15,929	. . .	14,419	10	. . .
7	19,674	20,439	15,723	25	30
9	. . .	24,558	19,105	. . .	29
11	. . .	29,221	23,324	. . .	25
12	. . .	35,271	27,947	. . .	26
13	. . .	42,927	33,583	. . .	28
14	. . .	52,382	39,626	. . .	32
15	. . .	60,743	47,116	. . .	29

Source: *Annual Report of the President's Pay Agent, 1980*, and *1981*.

Replacing personnel limits with stricter budget controls deserves at least an experimental test.

SALARY INCREASES. And now the pain. Splitting the general schedule makes no sense unless the salaries of the entry-level professionals and managers in the new professional and managerial service are then raised to market levels. In 1980 this would have required increased pay for professionals and managers in grade 5, for example, of about 26 percent (from $12,300 to the $15,500 level shown in the private sector by the BLS survey). Since there are only about 50,000 professionals and managerial workers in these grades, the budgetary costs would not be staggering. But rates of pay would have to be adjusted in higher grades as well to preserve some internal sense in the professional and managerial pay-rate structure.

The upper limits on salary increases that would be necessary to restore full comparability of salaries between the sectors can be found by comparing private enterprise pay rates in March 1981 with general schedule pay rates in March 1980 (table 4-5). An October 1980 pay hike that had raised the latter rates to the level of the former would have eliminated the time lag now built into the system as well as made up for the post-1976 hold-down in salary rates. To reach these upper limits by a one-time realignment of pay would require huge salary increases. Pay raises for entry-level professionals would be about 33 percent, and for upper-level professionals, 25 to 32 percent.

If the government made such a salary adjustment, it could then further simplify its annual pay adjustment system. Full-blown annual surveys of matched jobs would be unnecessary. Annual changes in the clerical and technical schedule and in the professional and managerial schedule could be set by changes in broad earnings indexes. The resources saved in the annual survey could then be channeled into ongoing studies of locality pay and of occupations meriting special rates. A full comparability survey would be needed periodically to determine whether there had been structural shifts in the nonfederal sector—but a five-year spacing would probably be adequate.

RSR and Pay Reform

The size of the salary increases apparently called for makes it imperative that pay reform and retirement reform be jointly established. If a "new hire" form of phasing in retirement reform was implemented, the large pay raises illustrated here should be reserved only for new hires. The logic is that new hires have signed on for jobs in which the retirement bonus has been eliminated and therefore deserve a full and fair salary rate. Other employees would not get such a salary boost because they would still be receiving a bloated retirement benefit. This arrangement would probably help the government's recruiting enormously but would not solve the problem of the too rapid retirement of experienced employees.

One way to implement both retirement and pay reforms more quickly suggests itself. The new retirement plan and the higher salary scale could initially be made available only to new hires, but existing employees could be admitted to the new pay system by voluntarily dropping their CSR rights in exchange for a "buyout." The buyout would consist of credit in the social security system for past work and a lump-sum payment into the RSR-IRA account equal to what the supplement would have been had the plan been in operation over the employee's past federal career.[45] Such a buyout would be a bargain for the government—by canceling much larger future liabilities—and it might be attractive to some employees given the size of the pay increases they would become eligible for. In any event, this proposal would be a noncoercive way to speed up the pace of compensation reform.

It is obvious that the proposal set out here for pay and retirement reform is amenable to compromise. Even with the universalization of social security coverage, a margin of advantage could be retained in the civil servants' retirement package over private sector plans, but such a compromise should entail a smaller one-time hike in salaries.[46] Such a moderate change might be viewed more favorably by high-earning civil servants, who would face a less abrupt change in compensation. But unless a major change is put into effect, the prospects of a budget-cutting Congress chipping away at federal employee compensation, often in unfair ways that generate quick budget savings, are all too real.

Conclusion

In this chapter I have reviewed two kinds of compensation reform proposals. The first, exemplified by President Carter's and President Reagan's pay reform legislation, was in large part budget-cutting masquerading as compensation reform. It could have disastrous effects on the quality of the federal work force as the current structural flaws are magnified. The second is a true reform package that costs the taxpayer money in the short run in exchange for significant long-term taxpayer savings and for an admittedly conjectural set of managerial improvements. Politicians ordinarily have much too high a discount rate to buy investments with such long-term payoffs. But in the realm of pay, and especially retirement pay, there is no sensible way to reform programs without taking a long view. Our tragic inability to cope with long-term problems in social security should make clear why foresight must be built into our political decisionmaking. This is no less true in considering the retirement for civil servants and complementary pay reform proposals that one hopes will be stimulated by this study.

45. Only the employer's share (of up to 7 percent) would be part of the buyout. The employee's past civil service retirement contributions would also have to be split between the social security fund and the RSR-IRA.

46. Some examples of such civil service retirement alternatives are set forth in Congressional Research Service, *Universal Social Security Coverage: Extending Mandatory Coverage*, Brief IB 80086 (GPO, 1980).

Appendix A

Slots versus Salaries and Expenses

FEDERAL agencies are usually subject to two important constraints on hiring employees. One is that each agency is allocated a limited budget to obligate for "salaries and expenses" (pay and fringe benefits, travel, office equipment, consultant fees, and the like). The second constraint is a ceiling on number of personnel. Until 1981 this "slot limit" was the number of permanent employees as of a particular date, but starting in 1981 the limit is the full-time equivalent number of workers during the fiscal year.[1] Almost all agencies claim that they are more constrained in their personnel decisions by the slot limit than by the salaries and expenses limit. That is, the agency typically runs up against its slot limit before it runs out of salary and expense money. As a result, some salary and expense money that cannot be spent for productive personnel purposes is spent for unnecessary (usually end-of-fiscal-year) purchases, such as low-priority consultant fees, more calculators and typewriters, and trips to distant field projects.[2] Finally, it is contended that since the slot limit treats all workers as equals, agencies tend to have too many chiefs and not enough run-of-the-mill native Americans. The result is upward grade creep, leading to higher payrolls for any given slot limit in the future. One widely favored (except in Congress) solution to these problems of government employment is to simply eliminate the slot constraint.[3] What follows is a simple model of the current procedure and an analysis of the effects of dropping the slot limit.

1. The new constraint is intended to eliminate the bias against part-time employees and to discourage the practice of "no hires" until after the settlement date in the old system.
2. The disadvantage of leaving funds unspent is well-known—it reduces the budget next year.
3. A report by the General Accounting Office, Comptroller General of the United States, *Improving the Credibility and Management of the Federal Workforce through Better Planning and Budgetary Controls*, FPCD 81-54 (GAO, 1981), is one of many reports reaching this conclusion.

FIGURE A-1. *Selection of the Mix of High-Grade and Low-Grade Employees under Alternative Constraints*

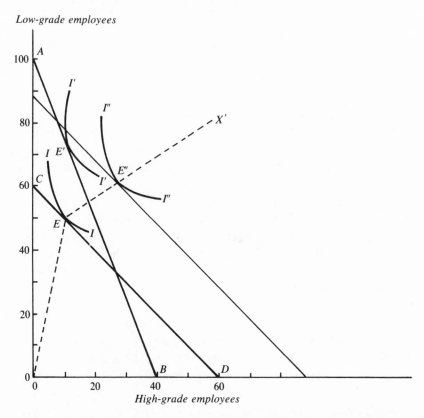

Low-grade employees

High-grade employees

Figure A-1 depicts how an agency might make its personnel decisions under the system of constraints described above. It is assumed that there are two grades of employee, "low" and "high," earning $10,000 and $25,000 a year, respectively. Suppose that after the agency has set aside some of its salary and expense budget for necessary nonsalary expenses, it has $1 million left. Then it can purchase any of the combinations of the two grades of labor along the line *AB* on the figure. But now additionally it is assumed that a personnel ceiling of sixty employees is imposed. This constraint is shown by line *CD*. Then the effective constraint on the agency is given by the line *CFB*.

The agency's ranking of points in the diagram is summarized by iso-output curves *II*, *I'I'*, and *I"I"*. Along any one such curve the agency's managers believe that the agency's "output" is constant. Their goal is to reach maximum output, the iso-output curve farthest from the origin, while remaining within budget and under the personnel ceiling. Output can mean actual delivery of service to the public, or it can mean that combination of employees that maximizes the agency head's career advancement—or anything else that might enter the agency's preference structure.

The statement that ordinarily a slot limit is binding on an agency's employment choice amounts to saying that it makes its employment decision under the dual constraint on line segment CF. This is illustrated by point E, where fifty units of low-grade labor and ten units of high-grade labor are hired. All the salary and expense money is not spent on personnel ($50 \times \$10,000 + 10 \times \$25,000 = \$750,000$); the rest goes into those extra typewriters and end-of-year contracts.

As the slot limit rises over time, the agency would expand along a path shown by the dashed line OEX. It seems plausible that OEX is concave from above as output rises, to indicate the economies of scale that occur as a relatively fixed cadre of managers (high-grade employees) is more effectively used. Above some output, however, OEX would become concave from below, as managers have to be hired to supervise and coordinate managers. In this range, agencies will choose a high-grade mix for their work force, as illustrated by the iso-output curve $I''I''$ reaching tangency with a line segment parallel to CD at a point like E'', where the high-to-low-grade employee ratio is higher than at E.[4]

If all these propositions are accepted as accurately reflecting past employment practice in the government sector, it is easy to analyze the effect of dropping the personnel ceiling. Returning to the initial equilibrium point E, suppose that the slot constraint CD is eliminated. The agency's new equilibrium position would be E'. In comparison with the original equilibrium,

1. total employment at E' must be higher;
2. the number of low-grade workers must be higher;
3. a larger proportion of salary and expense money must be used for salaries; and
4. the grade mix of employment may be higher, lower, or the same as originally.

4. In private sector output analysis, it is often assumed that a plant would never reach this scale. Once the point of diseconomies was reached, the firm would simply open a second plant or a competitor would. In the federal government these considerations would not apply—there will always be only one Social Security Administration.

The last result is the only one that is not intuitively obvious. The reason for the ambiguous conclusion about the effect of eliminating the personnel constraint on the grade mix is that, while the agency will take relative salaries into account at the margin (thus substituting more of the low-grade workers for the high-grade workers), it is also true that eliminating the personnel constraint in effect increases the purchasing power of the agency's salary and expense budget (AF is further out than CF). This increased purchasing power is used to raise output, an effect that increases demand for high-grade employees as well as for low-grade ones. Depending on which stage of scale economies the agency is operating under, this scale-of-output effect may overcome the substitution effect that flows from the agency's consideration of relative pay rates. In general, however, unless diseconomies of scale are very strong (and substitution effects very weak), the equilibrium without the slot limit would exhibit a lower average grade.

There are several advantages to dropping personnel limits. It would take away incentives for federal agencies to waste salary and expense funds (much more effectively than attempts at direct control over travel, consulting, and other uses of salary and expense budgets), and it would force agencies at the margin to recognize cost differences between workers.[5] It may not, however, be a sure cure for the upward drift in grade levels in the federal service.

5. Unfortunately, the charge made against agency budgets for contributions to the federal civil service retirement fund woefully understates the true costs of this fringe benefit. Moreover, the true cost of retirement may differ radically among the various grades of the civil service because of variations in career patterns.

Derivation of Civil Service Retirement Estimates in Table 3-5

1. *Estimation of final salary.* Since CSR provides an annuity whose *initial value* is based on the product of a *years of service factor* and the *high-3 average* salary, any one of these can be derived from the other two. In table 3-5 CSR data are provided for the initial annuity and for years of service. Thus for the first annuitant group shown, years of service equal 34.8, which corresponds to a years of service factor of 0.6585 (first 5.0 years at 0.0150 a year, next 5.0 years at 0.0175 a year, and next 24.8 years at 0.0200 a year). Since the initial annuity is $15,429, the high-3 average salary must be $15,429 ÷ 0.6585 = $23,431. Assuming that the highest three years of salary were the final three and that salary grew at an average annual rate of 8.8 percent (Board of Actuaries assumption), the final year's salary would be approximately 1.088 times the high-3 average, or $23,431 × 1.088 = $25,492.

2. *Estimation of CSR wealth accumulated at retirement.* CSR provides an annuity (A), indexed to the consumer price index. The present value (W) of the annuity (I assume single life throughout) depends on the life expectancy of the retiree (n), the rate of inflation (p), and the nominal interest rate (r). In fact, such an indexed annuity is the equivalent of a bond with maturity n, equal annual payments A, and real interest i ($= r - p$). The present value of such a bond is

$$W = \left[\frac{(1 + i)^n - 1}{i(1 + i)^n} \right] A.$$

If, as the Board of Actuaries assumes, $p = 0.06$, $r = 0.07$, and therefore $i = 0.01$, the ratio term in the equation is equal to 18.29 for $n = 20.3$ years, the life expectancy of a person retiring at 59.1 years (the top group of optional retirees in table 3-5).[1] Since A equals $15,429 for this group, $W = $282,196. All entries in table 3-5 were derived in a similar way.

1. Life expectancy for all races and all sexes from Bureau of the Census, *Statistical Abstract of the United States: 1979* (Government Printing Office, 1980), p. 71. Vital

3. *Estimation of fraction of employee's pay required to fund CRS wealth.* Suppose a person put aside the same fraction (k) of his salary each year into a retirement fund earning an annual nominal interest rate r. Suppose that the work life was m years long and that salary grew smoothly at the rate of w a year. In the first year the worker earns S dollars and contributes kS to the fund. By retirement, m years later, this initial contribution has grown to

$$kS(1 + r)^{m-1} \text{ in year } m.$$

In the second year wages have grown by a factor of $1 + w$, but the contribution of $kS(1 + w)$ earns interest for one less year and grows to

$$kS(1 + w)^1(1 + r)^{m-2} \text{ in year } m.$$

The final salary (F) is $S(1 + w)^{m-1}$, and the contribution (assumed to be made at the end of the year) does not earn interest by year m:

$$kS(1 + w)^{m-1}.$$

The wealth (W) of the fund in year m is the sum of these accumulations, which can be stated as a geometric series with first term $kS(1 + w)^{m-1}$ and common factor $(1 + r)/(1 + w)$. Its sum is given by

$$[kS(1 + w)^{m-1}] \left[1 - \left(\frac{1 + r}{1 + w} \right)^m \middle/ 1 - \left(\frac{1 + r}{1 + w} \right) \right].$$

Therefore,

$$W = kF \left[1 - \left(\frac{1 + r}{1 + w} \right)^m \middle/ 1 - \left(\frac{1 + r}{1 + w} \right) \right].$$

For $r = 0.070$ and $w = 0.088$, as assumed by the Board of Actuaries,[2] the last ratio term equals 26.62 for the first group in table 3-5 whose $m = 34.8$ years. Given the estimates for final salary and CSR wealth shown above, I solve for k in the last equation:

$$282{,}196 = k(25{,}492)(26.62), \text{ or } k = 0.416.$$

---

statistics are from 1977. For the other groups in table 3-5, life expectancy is 19.2, 16.4, and 16.4 years, respectively.

2. These are the board's assumptions for the future, not for the past. But by use of their assumptions, my calculations are comparable to the future normal cost estimates of the board.

TABLE B-1. *Annuity as Fraction of Final Salary, by Years of Service and Final Three-Year Wage Growth Assumptions*

Years of service	Annuity as fraction of final salary	
	No wage growth in final three years	10 percent wage growth in final three years
10	0.1625	0.1482
20	0.3625	0.3305
25	0.4625	0.4217
30	0.5625	0.5129
35	0.6625	0.6041
40	0.7625	0.6953

This is the ratio in the last column of table 3-5. Other entries were derived by the same procedure.

4. *Sensitivity of estimates.* The amount of initial annuity under CSR depends on years of service and high-3 average salary. The relation of the annuity to *final* pay depends on wage growth in the last three years of the career (assuming those years to be the high-3 ones). The initial annuity expressed as a fraction of final salary (replacement rate) at two alternative assumptions about salary growth in the last three years of the career is shown in table B-1.

The amount of CSR wealth required to fund an annual annuity of $1 (adjusted each year for inflation) depends on the life expectancy of the annuitant and the real interest rate (nominal rate minus inflation rate) as shown in table B-2.

The fraction of annual salary that would have to be set aside in an accumulation fund to yield various multiples of final salary depends on the length of career and on the rate of growth of salary compared with the rate of interest (that is, on $w - r$). Table B-3 shows these relations.

These values are related as follows. Let A equal the indexed annuity, F be equal to final salary, and W be the wealth accumulated at retirement. Then A/F (table B-1) times W/A (table B-2) equals W/F (table B-3). Thus, for example, if one wants to determine the cost of funding civil service retirement for a person with forty years of service who retires at an age where life expectancy is fifteen years, the high-low estimates could be derived in the following way.

High: from table B-1, $A/F = 0.7625$;

from table B-2, at real interest rate of 0.5, $W/A = 14.4$;

therefore, $W/F = 10.98$;

TABLE B-2. *Wealth Required to Fund an Indexed Annuity of One Dollar, by Life Expectancy and Real Interest Rates*
Dollars

Life expectancy	Real interest rate				
	0	0.5	1.0	1.5	2.0
25	25.0	23.4	22.0	20.7	19.5
20	20.0	19.0	18.0	17.2	16.4
15	15.0	14.4	13.9	13.3	12.8
10	10.0	9.7	9.5	9.2	9.0

TABLE B-3. *Fraction of Annual Salary Required to Produce Wealth at Retirement of Various Multiples of Final Salary, by Years of Service and Alternative Levels of Salary Growth Less Interest Rates*

Years of service	Multiples of final salary				
	12	10	8	5	2
	$w - r = 0.02$[a]				
40	0.42	0.36	0.29	0.18	0.07
35	0.47	0.39	0.32	0.20	0.08
30	0.53	0.44	0.35	0.22	0.09
20	0.72	0.60	0.48	0.30	0.12
10	1.31	1.09	0.87	0.55	0.22
	$w - r = 0.01$[a]				
40	0.36	0.30	0.24	0.15	0.06
35	0.40	0.33	0.27	0.17	0.07
30	0.46	0.38	0.31	0.18	0.08
20	0.66	0.55	0.44	0.27	0.11
10	1.25	1.05	0.84	0.52	0.21

a. Rate of salary growth is w; rate of interest is r..

from table B-3, for $W/F = 11$, and assuming $w - r = 0.02$, the fraction of annual salary that must be saved is 0.39.

Low: from table B-1, $A/F = 0.6953$;
from table B-2, at real interest of 2.0, $W/A = 12.8$;
therefore, $W/F = 8.9$;
from table B-3, for $W/F = 9$, and $w - r = 0.01$, the fraction of salary that must be set aside is 0.27.

Thus, even for a given number of years of service and age at retirement, the cost of CSR could vary considerably (27 to 39 percent of own pay, in this case) depending on the real interest rate and the excess of real wage growth over the real interest rate that are assumed.

Index

Library of Congress Cataloging in Publication data:

Hartman, Robert W.
  Pay and pensions for federal workers.
  Includes bibliographical references and index.
  1. United States—Officials and employees—Salaries, allowances, etc.   2. Civil service pensions—United States.   I. Title.
JK776.H36   1983   353.001′23   82-45980
ISBN 0-8157-3496-4
ISBN 0-8157-3495-6 (pbk.)